T0318919

Cambridge Elements ☰

Elements in Construction Grammar
edited by
Thomas Hoffmann
Catholic University of Eichstätt-Ingolstadt
Alexander Bergs
Osnabrück University

COPILOTS FOR LINGUISTS

AI, Constructions, and Frames

Tiago Timponi Torrent
Federal University of Juiz de Fora
Thomas Hoffmann
*Catholic University of Eichstätt-Ingolstadt/
Hunan Normal University*
Arthur Lorenzi Almeida
Federal University of Juiz de Fora
Mark Turner
Case Western Reserve University

CAMBRIDGE
UNIVERSITY PRESS

Shaftesbury Road, Cambridge CB2 8EA, United Kingdom

One Liberty Plaza, 20th Floor, New York, NY 10006, USA

477 Williamstown Road, Port Melbourne, VIC 3207, Australia

314–321, 3rd Floor, Plot 3, Splendor Forum, Jasola District Centre,
New Delhi – 110025, India

103 Penang Road, #05–06/07, Visioncrest Commercial, Singapore 238467

Cambridge University Press is part of Cambridge University Press & Assessment,
a department of the University of Cambridge.

We share the University's mission to contribute to society through the pursuit of
education, learning and research at the highest international levels of excellence.

www.cambridge.org
Information on this title: www.cambridge.org/9781009475907

DOI: 10.1017/9781009439190

First published 2023

A catalogue record for this publication is available from the British Library

ISBN 978-1-009-47590-7 Hardback
ISBN 978-1-009-43922-0 Paperback
ISSN 2753-2674 (online)
ISSN 2753-2666 (print)

Additional resources for this publication at www.cambridge.org/copilots_resources

Cambridge University Press & Assessment has no responsibility for the persistence
or accuracy of URLs for external or third-party internet websites referred to in this
publication and does not guarantee that any content on such websites is, or will
remain, accurate or appropriate.

Copilots for Linguists

AI, Constructions, and Frames

Elements in Construction Grammar

DOI: 10.1017/9781009439190

First published online: December 2023

Tiago Timponi Torrent
Federal University of Juiz de Fora

Thomas Hoffmann
Catholic University of Eichstätt-Ingolstadt/Hunan Normal University

Arthur Lorenzi Almeida
Federal University of Juiz de Fora

Mark Turner
Case Western Reserve University

Author for correspondence: Tiago Timponi Torrent, tiago.torrent@ufjf.br

Abstract: Artificial intelligence (AI) can assist the linguist in doing research on the structure of language. This Element illustrates this possibility by showing how a conversational AI based on a large language model (AI LLM chatbot) can assist the construction grammarian, and especially the frame semanticist. An AI LLM chatbot is a text-generation system trained on vast amounts of text. To generate text, it must be able to find patterns in the data and mimic some linguistic capacity, at least in the eyes of a cooperative human user. The Element does not focus on whether AIs "understand" language. Rather, it investigates whether AI LLM chatbots are useful tools for linguists. The discussion is reframed from what AI LLM chatbots can do with language to what they can do for linguists. The Element finds that a chatty LLM can labor usefully as an eliciting interlocutor and presents precise, scripted routines for prompting conversational LLMs.

This Element also has a video abstract: www.cambridge.org/copilots_abstract

Keywords: Construction Grammar, AI, large language model, FrameNet, linguistics

ISBNs: 9781009475907 (HB), 9781009439220 (PB), 9781009439190 (OC)
ISSNs: 2753-2674 (online), 2753-2666 (print)

Contents

Introduction

Artificial intelligence (AI) has recently produced one generative system after another, trained on language, photos, videos, music, and other forms of multi-modal communication, and it is sure to continue these advances at a brisk pace. These AI generative systems produce forms such as texts or pictures. Construction grammarians investigate the exact ways in which such forms prompt for meaning. To what extent can the construction grammarian draw on these AI systems to study constructions – that is, form–meaning pairs – and to investigate the ways that constructions blend to create constructs, where by "constructs" we mean communicative performances?

Consider large language models (LLMs), which derive from mathematical models that rely on self-supervised training on enormous amounts of data in a deep neural network architecture (Bommasani et al., 2021). Natural Language Processing (NLP) research has strenuously investigated whether LLMs can represent different aspects of linguistic knowledge (see Rogers et al., 2020 for a survey of 150 publications). The present Element asks quite a different question about the relation of LLMs and linguistics. Instead of focusing on whether LLMs have any understanding of language or not, it asks whether LLMs can be useful tools for doing linguistics. Linguists have historically used many digital assistants as copilots for research. Can AI, specifically conversational LLMs, join that list? We reframe the discussion about chatty LLMs from what they can do with language to what they can do for linguists. Our goal is to show how linguists can "find a way to benefit from conversational AI without losing the many important aspects that render scientific work one of the most profound and gratifying enterprises: curiosity, imagination and discovery" (van Dis et al., 2023: 226).

In this Element, we conducted our experiments using two AI LLM chatbots: one proprietary and one open source. The proprietary chatbot was ChatGPT by OpenAI, often running the GPT4 model. To locate a suitable open source alternative, we ran preliminary tests with Alpaca, Koala, OpenchatKit, and OpenAssistant. For OpenAssistant, we used the HuggingChat interface. Although we trained OpenchatKit on a high-performance 80GB GPU node, its performance was not competitive. OpenAssistant, without any additional training from us, performed the best of these open source alternatives. Accordingly, we conducted the same experiments using both ChatGPT and OpenAssistant.

The possibilities for AI LLM chatbots as eliciting interlocutors for linguists are extensive. The conversational interface allows for continuous dialogue with the system, which can present text in a variety of formats, including formats ideal for further computational processing. For example, AI LLM chatbots can write code that is useful for the linguist. When informed of mistakes, they can respond repeatedly and inventively to requests for corrections. In this Element, we investigate whether these chatbots can aid the construction grammarian. Since Frame Semantics is the central theory of meaning in cognitive Construction Grammar approaches, our most specific investigation explores whether AI LLM chatbots can aid the frame semanticist in expanding and refining FrameNet – the major, global computational repository of representations of frames, devised at its inception to serve as an aid to linguists.

For the LLM-based chatbot to generate text accepted as mimicking human language (including false, mistaken, biased, and offensive content), its output must draw on its exposure to vast oceans of text; it must mimic the use of cognitive frames and grammatical patterns, regardless of whether it is saying things that are true or false, biased or objective, naughty or nice. Otherwise, no one would understand it; it would not merely say things with which we might disagree, things we might find distasteful, things we might judge to be contrary to fact, but, incomparably more important for the work of the linguist, it would say things that are linguistically *alien, nonhuman*.

The mimicking ability of these chatbots depends on three factors. First and foremost, it depends on the human user's ability to construe meaning from linguistic forms. The human user can take the stance that the entity responsible for producing those forms is cooperatively engaging in a communicative effort. Second, it depends on the vector probabilistic representations (embeddings) that LLMs build for linguistic forms during training. Its representations are based on the recognition of patterns in hundreds of billions of words in the training data (Brown et al., 2020; Touvron et al., 2023). Lastly, it depends on the fine-tuning of the LLM through reinforcement learning from human feedback, improving the overall quality of the conversational interface by reducing toxicity and hallucinations, and increasing trustworthiness and perceived appropriateness. Given that an important part of the job of linguists in general – and of construction grammarians and frame semanticists in particular – involves analyzing data and recognizing usage patterns in language, it is plausible that an AI LLM chatbot can assist the linguist in finding and detailing those patterns.

A native speaker shows astounding mastery of a language, but has very little conscious understanding of the processes and knowledge underlying that mastery. Those processes and knowledge are in the backstage of cognition, mostly hidden from consciousness. The linguist is forever attempting to drag onstage a little of that backstage system. This is a notoriously difficult occupation. The linguist must first notice some hint of an element of a grammatical system, and then work, often for decades, on the details. Fillmore and colleagues (1988:

518–519), for example, explain that after working for months on the "let alone construction," during which all evidence seemed to suggest that it was a negative polarity construction, they began to encounter solid ranges of attested examples of non-negative *let alone*. It then took them more months to arrive at an "exploratory speculation" of the underlying principles of non-negative *let alone*. It is common for the linguist to notice a linguistic phenomenon consciously only after long exposure to usage, and then to work on that topic for years. Might an AI LLM chatbot serve *not* as an expert or even a reliable informant but instead as a tool for *eliciting* knowledge and insight from the linguist? Can it suggest analyses that prompt the linguist to better analyses? To be sure, all the examples we will give in the following sections show the ELIZA effect: "the susceptibility of people to read far more understanding than is warranted into strings of symbols – especially words – strung together by computers" (Hofstader, 1995: 157). The computational tool may produce output that the tool does not understand at all but that the *human being* finds meaningful and useful. The ELIZA effect consists of attributing that *understanding* to the tool. Here, we are interested, on the contrary, in only whether the tool might be *useful* to the linguist, whose job is to recognize patterns on which, as it conveniently happens, the tool has been elaborately trained.

1 Safety Instructions: Risks and Limitations of LLMs and Generative AI

Before taking off with our new copilot, it is necessary, however, to consider the limitations of the current approach and to post some warnings. A substantial amount of research has focused on the limits of LLMs in understanding language (Bender & Koller, 2020; Mahowald et al., 2023) and on their potential risks (Ruane et al., 2019; Bender et al., 2021; Birhane et al., 2021). Moreover, LLMs only model the probabilities that a given word follows a preceding string of words. These probabilities are a function of the "weights" assigned to nodes in the machine learning model. The weights are created by training the model on very large amounts of existing textual data, sometimes modified by further reinforcement learning through human feedback (RLHF), during which the human user provides feedback on the actual performance of the LLM, so as to adjust its reward function and therefore fine-tune its subsequent performance. Accordingly, generative AI services like ChatGPT that depend on LLMs will generate text depending on their training data. It is in the nature of the process that training an LLM on unimaginably vast oceans of texts will produce output that follows the linguistic patterns of the training data. But – a quite different subject – it will also produce content whose truth-value follows the truth-value of the training data. If the assertions and claims of the training data are garbage, the product will most probably be garbage. Output that is linguistically perfect can prompt for meanings that are totally false, just as a con artist can be a master of communication. In addition, there is an extra threat to reliability, referred to as "confabulation" or "hallucination": The LLM will mostly do as commanded, generating text according to the user's prompting, which naturally carries the user's preferences. Confabulation can contribute to the production of text that is factually unreliable. Many analysts have warned that to use a generative AI unreflectively as it comes out of the box is to use it wrong. For example, the personal tech columnist for *The New York Times* writes:

> The chatbots are the least beneficial when we ask them questions and then hope whatever answers they come up with on their own are true, which is how they were designed to be used. But when directed to use information from trusted sources, such as credible websites and research papers, A.I. can carry out helpful tasks with a high degree of accuracy. (Chen, 2023)

For the future, what seems to be required in order to create a reliable reference resource for linguistics is to train LLMs on texts and/or databases regarded as authoritative (e.g., FrameNet or https://constructicon.de/). For example, we used AskYourPDF to fine-tune ChatGPT (using the GPT4 model) on the pdf of a classic, long, technical CxG article by Fillmore, Kay, and O'Connor, "Regularity and idiomaticity." The result is a chatbot that delivers answers to questions about that article. Training generative AI to serve as a reliable inform- ant or tutor for linguistics is not the subject of the present Element, but it is important for readers to remember that ChatGPT and other generative AIs cannot be assumed to have been trained on reliable information only.

Finally, Birhane and colleagues (2023), in a *Nature* Viewpoint interview paper, list key risks associated with the use of chatty LLMs such as ChatGPT and OpenAssistant in scientific practice. On top of the known issues regarding the carbon footprint of such models and the poor labor conditions involved in training some of them, the authors point out that LLMs are tools and must always be regarded as such. In Birhane's words, "science is a human enterprise and LLMs are tools – albeit impressive at predicting the next word in a sequence based on previously 'seen' words – with limitations such as brittleness (suscep- tibility to catastrophic failure), unreliability and the fabrication of seemingly 'scientific' nonsense." Leslie, another author of the *Nature* Viewpoint article, claims that:

> Scientists must view LLMs and GenAI technologies as exploratory tools that bolster responsible, mission-driven and society-led research practices and that support the advancement of scientific discovery and understanding. To

paraphrase the words of economist Zvi Griliches, the expanding use of these AI technologies in scientific research is the "discovery of a method of discovery" – the invention of a new set of research tools that support and enable new pathways of insight, innovation and ingenuity. (Birhane et al., 2023: 278)

In line with this, the current Element tries to showcase how AI LLM chatbots can be used responsibly and productively for Frame Semantic and Construction Grammar research. Towards the end, we will return to the issue of reliability and brittleness of this method and assess it in the light of the findings of our experiments.

2 Constructions

Various construction grammarians come at language from various different vantage points. These include typology, language acquisition, cognitive mechanisms, formalization, and computational implementation. Consequently, different Construction Grammar approaches, with different emphases, have emerged. These approaches include Radical Construction Grammar, Cognitive Construction Grammar, Embodied Construction Grammar, Fluid Construction Grammar, and Sign-Based Construction Grammar. They often differ on important theoretical assumptions (cf., e.g., Hoffmann & Trousdale, 2013; Hoffmann, 2022a: 256; Ungerer & Hartmann, 2023). What unites all constructionist approaches is that they agree that language is nonmodular, without derivations, and that the central units of language are constructions (form–meaning pairs). All construction grammarians aspire to account for creativity otherwise ignored in linguistics. In doing so, they follow the wisdom of the study of σχήματα (schemata) in classical rhetoric (Turner, 1998): σχῆμα was a technical term used to signify a conventional pairing of a form and a meaning (a construction) or, more broadly, a form and a conceptual pattern. To know a language, one must know its *schemata* and how they can be used and combined creatively. Of course, as both classical rhetoric and Construction Grammar recognize, nearly all creativity in networks of form–meaning pairs goes unnoticed in consciousness by individuals, despite what in retrospect is clearly very rapid development, innovation, and extension.

The meaning side of a form–meaning pair is often a cognitive frame. Human beings think largely by using mental operations they already possess to work on conceptual arrays they already know. Some of their knowledge is organized into mental bundles that we call "mental frames," "cognitive frames," or just "frames" (Fillmore, 1968, 1976, 1977a, 1977b, 1982, 1985, 2008, 2013; Fillmore & Atkins, 1992, 1994; Fillmore et al., 1988; Lowe et al., 1997). Some of these frames are so important to communication that we expect every mature native speaker of a particular language to have mastered them, or at least a version of them. The language presupposes their availability to its speakers. For example, when someone says, "I have to call my stockbroker," everyone can activate the appropriate mental package, the appropriate conceptual bundle of related elements. We imagine, unless we are told or have reason to believe otherwise, that the telephone call is about *buying and selling securities*. Nobody needs to explain that the call is about buying and selling securities, because the word "stockbroker" calls up that frame. To understand "I have to call my stockbroker," we activate information from that frame to build a small mental array containing the speaker, the phone call, and the broker. In the frame for *buying and selling securities*, there is a role for the agent who initiates the trade in a financial market, and we understand that the stockbroker is in that role. In that frame, there is an actual client, who owns the securities, and we place the speaker in that role. In that frame, the client communicates with the agent, and we take "call" to indicate a phone call between the client and the agent. Of course, other interpretations of "I have to call my stockbroker" are possible. If the speaker then calls out to someone walking by in the park, we might have to reframe the utterance to reach a compatible interpretation. Such forced reframing can be funny, exactly because the speaker seemed to invite us to use one frame (communicating with an agent to transact a buy–sell transaction for securities), but then forced a shift in the frame to *calling out to get the attention of someone*. Forced frame shifts are often a source of humor (Coulson, 2001).

Forms of all sorts can evoke frames: pointing (at the policeman or the waiter), paintings and sculptures and pictures of objects (the holy grail, a sword, a bagpipe), melodies (the leitmotif for Darth Vader), and so on. The most obvious forms that evoke frames are words, or, more precisely, lexical units. Consider *safe*, for example, said of some situation. It prompts us to activate a mental web corresponding to that situation, activate a frame of potential *harm*, and understand that the situation with *harm* is counterfactual to the mental space in which *safe* applies.[1] A single sentence can contain many such words, activating many such frames, as in the National Public Radio warning a few days before Halloween, October 2000: "A *Halloween costume* that *limits sight*

---

[1] Actually, *safe* can evoke two different frames, depending on its constructional context: In *a child-safe beach* it activates the **Being_at_risk** frame, resulting in an interpretation in which the beach is seen as a location in which the child is "protected from or not exposed to danger or risk; not likely to be harmed or lost" (https://framenet2.icsi.berkeley.edu/fnReports/data/lu/lu12444.xml?mode=lexentry). In contrast to this, *a shark-safe beach* triggers the **Risky_situation** frame and entails that the beach is a place where sharks are "not likely to lead to harm or injury" (https://framenet2.icsi.berkeley.edu/fnReports/data/lu/lu13377.xml?mode=lexentry). Which of the two frames is activated, obviously, depends crucially on our encyclopedic world-knowledge.

or *movement* is an *accident lurking* in *disguise*." (*Halloween* will activate all activities and props associated with the holiday, including types of *costumes*, trick-and-treating, and so on. *Sight* and *movement* evoke embodied frames, including the fact that they can be temporarily impeded. *Accident* activates the catastrophe frame and *lurking* a frame of hiding. Finally, *disguise* is intentionally used ambiguously here, activating the frame of a potentially negative effect that is masked as something positive as well as evoking the *costume* element of the Halloween frame.)

Syntactic patterns, so-called argument structure constructions (Goldberg, 1995, 2006, 2019), also evoke frames of basic human event construals such as transfer, movement, or causation. The syntax is the form; the frame is part of the meaning evoked. A verb like THROW (e.g., *He threw the ball towards the pitcher*) evokes the frame of Caused_motion and encodes the meaning of "propel[ing an object] with force through the air by a rapid movement of the arm and hand."[2] However, when such a verb is blended with the Ditransitive construction (FORM: NP_1 $Verb_2$ NP_3 NP_4 ↔ MEANING: $Agent_1$ causes $Recipient_3$ to receive $Patient_4$ by $Verb_2$-ing; adapted from Hoffmann, 2022a: 189), as in *She threw me the coke bottle*, the Transfer frame is activated by the argument structure construction in addition to the Caused_motion frame with which THROW is associated. Similarly, FLOAT prototypically activates the Motion frame, meaning "mov[ing] slowly or hover[ing] in a liquid or the air."[3] When combined with the Caused Motion construction (FORM: NP_1 $Verb_2$ NP_3 PP_4 ↔ MEANING: $Agent_1$ causes $Theme_3$ to move towards $Goal_4$ by $Verb_2$-ing; adapted from Hoffmann, 2022a: 187), the abstract syntactic construction adds the Caused Motion meaning to the simple movement meaning of FLOAT: *He floated the boat to me* (cf. Goldberg, 1995; Fauconnier & Turner, 1996, 2002; Turner, 2015). As recent studies have shown, argument structure constructions are not stored entirely independent of verbal predicates. Instead, there are strong usage ties between certain verbs and these abstract constructions (e.g., GIVE, TELL, SEND, ASK, and SHOW and the Ditransitive construction; Stefanowitsch, 2013: 293; cf. also Boas, 2005, 2013: 237–238; Perek & Lemmens, 2010; Croft, 2012: 364–374; Herbst, 2018). This makes frame-based analyses (see Section 5) a central topic for constructional research.

Constructions, symbolic pairings of form and meaning, range from morphological templates (e.g., FORM: un_1-$Verb_2$ ↔ MEANING: $reverse_1$ $Verb_2$-ing event; adapted from Hoffmann and Bergs, 2024) over word constructions (e.g., FORM:

---

[2]   https://framenet2.icsi.berkeley.edu/fnReports/data/lu/lu960.xml?mode=lexentry.
[3]   https://framenet2.icsi.berkeley.edu/fnReports/data/lu/lu6261.xml?mode=lexentry.

THROW ↔ MEANING: Cause_Motion frame | 'propel with force through the air by a rapid movement of the arm and hand') to abstract constructions such as the Ditransitive construction or the Caused Motion construction. One of the most thoroughly analyzed abstract constructions whose meaning is an elaborate prompt for blending a frame with another input space is the "X is the Y of Z" construction (XYZ) (e.g., *Death is the mother of beauty*, *These fire retardants are the asbestos of our time*; Turner, 1987). The construction has as its form the pattern NP$_1$ BE *the* NP$_2$ *of* NP$_3$ with each NP providing frame information that must be compressed via conceptual blending in the speaker's working memory: NP$_1$ (X) and NP$_3$ (Z) are combined into an input space (*death* and *beauty*/*fire retardants* and *our time*), while NP$_2$ (Y) activates a frame that is used to establish the relationship between X and Y that the speaker tries to express. Through conceptual blending, the construction then can give rise to a concise (sometimes metaphorical) meaning, such as that death, like a mother, "gives birth" to beauty, because our recognition of mortality is the basis of our reaction to beauty, or that fire retardants today are as frequently used, yet as secretly dangerous, as asbestos was as a building material in the 1960s and 1970s.

The XYZ construction is a clausal construction with a complex meaning pole that requires the spontaneous blending of various frames. In addition to argument structure constructions and clause-level constructions such as the XYZ construction, some researchers have recently suggested that there are even larger, schematic discourse-level constructions. Hoffmann and Bergs (2015, 2018, 2024 and references therein), for example, have provided evidence that football chants, *Knock Knock* jokes, and even TED talks can be analyzed as schematic constructions.

This section has illustrated the range of constructions that are analyzed within current constructionist research. The selection of the phenomena discussed in this section is obviously somewhat eclectic – for a more in-depth overview of the scope of present Construction Grammar research see, for example, Hoffmann and Trousdale (2013), Hilpert (2019), and Hoffmann (2022a). In the next section, we will outline how AI LLM chatbots can assist in constructionist research, using the constructions discussed in this section for our case studies.

3 Using an AI to Help Study Constructions

One can prompt an AI LLM chatbot to provide further examples and even analyses of such constructions. Starting with the *un*-VERB construction (see also Hoffmann, unpublished data[4]), one can, for example, prompt ChatGPT and OpenAssistant to give ten examples of the construction:

---

[4] Hoffmann, T. ChatGPT and CxG: The end or future of constructionist research and teaching?

(1)   USER: Hi, Assistant. The un-VERB construction which creates verbs such as e.g. "unbutton" or "untie" has a form that consist of "un" followed by a verb. The meaning of the construction is "reversal". Thus, "unbutton" means "to reverse a buttoning action" and "untie" means "to reverse a tying action." Please give 10 more examples of this construction.

(2)   a. ChatGPT: Sure, here are 10 more examples of the "un-verb" construction:
  1. Unzip – to reverse a zipping action
  2. Unfold – to reverse a folding action
  3. Unplug – to reverse a plugging action
  4. Unlock – to reverse a locking action
  5. Unwind – to reverse a winding action
  6. Uncork – to reverse a corking action
  7. Untangle – to reverse a tangling action
  8. Unlace – to reverse a lacing action
  9. Unravel – to reverse a unraveling action
  10. Unclasp – to reverse a clasping action
  I hope these examples are helpful!

  b. OpenAssistant: Here are ten additional examples of the un-verb construction in English:
  1. Unbuckle: To reverse an action of buckling
  2. Undraw: To reverse an action of drawing
  3. Unfold: To reverse an action of folding
  4. Uneven: To reverse an even number
  5. Understand: To reverse an action of understanding
  6. Untwist: To reverse an action of twisting
  7. Unbraid: To reverse an action of braiding
  8. Unpack: To reverse an action of packing
  9. Undo: To reverse any previous action or decision
  10. Unlike: To reverse your opinion or feeling towards someone or something

The ChatGPT results (2a) are generally good, but already showcase how a particular prompt crucially influences the model's output: In the prompt, the meaning of the construction is specified as "reversal" and the two examples given are "to reverse a buttoning action" and "to reverse a tying action." Just like conservative learners, the models generalize this to the pattern "to reverse a V-ing action," which they apply to all ten examples. As a result, they fail to report polysemous meanings (in addition to the meaning in (1), *unwind*, inter alia, has the figurative meaning "[t]o relieve from tension or anxiety, to cause to relax"[5]). Somewhat unexpected, however, is the fact that ChatGPT gives "to reverse a **un**raveling action" as the meaning of *unravel*. In all other cases, just as in the prompt, the models seem to strip the *un*-V word of its *un*-prefix in the meaning definitions (cf. *zipping*, *folding*, *plugging*, etc.). A potential reason

---

[5] www.oed.com/view/Entry/219600

might be that the model is affected by the frequency of the *un*-V word and the corresponding V word. Now, the precise content of the training data is not known, so as a proxy we queried the frequency of the verb lemma UNVERB_v* and VERB_* for the ten ChatGPT examples from (2) in the Corpus of Contemporary American English (COCA).

Currently, COCA comprises about one billion words – only a fraction of ChatGPT's training data. Moreover, just like ChatGPT's output, the numbers in Table 1 do not distinguish the various polysemous meanings of the V lemmas. Still, as expected, for all but two words, the V lemma is (considerably) more frequent than the *un*-V lemma. *Uncork* is 3.15 times more frequent than *cork* in COCA – –but both appear fairly infrequently (384 vs 121 tokens). In contrast to this, *unravel* is considerably more frequent than *ravel*, with a ratio of 76.06 to 1, and *ravel* appears only fifty-four times in COCA. Moreover, LLMs are, obviously, crucially influenced by the size of their training data. In this case, however, it seems as if this can even lead to implausible meaning descriptions (such as "to reverse a unraveling action" for *unravel*).

OpenAssistant (2b) arguably performs worse for this prompt: *Understand* is, of course, a highly frequent word, but does not segment into *un-* and *derstand*. Since *derstand* does not exist as a verb, this result is somewhat unexpected (and raises questions as to how well the prompt conduced OpenAssistant to perform the task). In addition to that, *uneven* as a verb is highly infrequent and means "to

Table 1 Frequency of *un*-V versus V lemma constructions for ChatGPT examples.

un-V lemma	Frequency	V lemma	Frequency	Ratio *un*-V lemma versus V lemma
UNZIP	1,411	ZIP	5,012	1 : 3.55
UNFOLD	12,727	FOLD	16,148	1 : 1.27
UNPLUG	973	PLUG	10,332	1 : 10.61
UNLOCK	9,097	LOCK	43,093	1 : 4.74
UNWIND	2,067	WIND	26,183	1 : 12.67
UNCORK	384	CORK	121	3.15 : 1
UNTANGLE	877	TANGLE	2,568	1 : 2.93
UNLACE	163	LACE	3,171	1 : 19.45
UNRAVEL	4,107	RAVEL	54	76.06 : 1
UNCLASP	60	CLASP	3,212	1 : 53.53

Table 2 Frequency of *un*-V versus V lemma constructions for OpenAssistant examples.

un-V lemma	Frequency	V lemma	Frequency	Ratio *un*-V lemma vs V lemma
UNBUCKLE	233	BUCKLE	4,049	1 : 17.38
UNDRAW	0	DRAW	135,022	N/A
UNFOLD	12,727	FOLD	16,148	1 : 1.27
UNEVEN	0	EVEN	1,645	N/A
*UNDERSTAND	N/A	N/A	N/A	N/A
UNTWIST	0	TWIST	16,274	N/A
UNBRAID	1	BRAID	1,351	1 : 1,351
UNPACK	3,248	PACK	35,348	1 : 10.88
UNDO	8,067	DO	8,186,409	1 : 1,014.80
UNLIKE	0	LIKE	614,689	N/A

make uneven,"[6] and not "to reverse an even number." At the same time, as Table 2 shows, OpenAssistant's examples are mostly ones for which the base V LEMMA is highly frequent (while several *un*-V lemmas such as *undraw*, *untwist*, or *unlike* do not appear even once in COCA).

Let us move along the lexicon–syntax cline and see how the LLMs deal with argument structure constructions:

(3)　　USER: Hi, Assistant. In the caused-motion frame, an agent performs an action on an object that causes it to move in a direction. "Throw" is a caused-motion verb. "Throw" evokes the caused-motion frame. "Throw" indicates that the subject of the verb performed an action, throwing, that caused an object to move in a direction. But the syntactic pattern "Noun Phrase – Verb Phrase – Noun Phrase – Prepositional Phrase" can also evoke the caused-motion frame. When it does, the verb can be intransitive. "She rolled the ball to me" does not mean that she actually rolled; instead, it indicates that she performed some action, whatever it was, that caused the ball to move in a direction in a rolling manner. "He slid the plate across the table to me" uses the intransitive verb "slide." In this sentence, the subject, "he," did not actually move across the table, but instead performed an action that caused the plate to move in a direction across the table, indicated by the prepositional phrase "to me." Please give 20 examples of intransitive verbs used in caused-motion clausal syntactic patterns, like "He floated the boat to me."

---

[6] www.oed.com/view/Entry/213004

(4)   a. ChatGPT: Certainly, here are examples of intransitive verbs used in caused-motion clausal syntactic patterns.
1.   She dreamed the car into the garage.
2.   They paused the game for a bathroom break.
3.   The child smiled the balloon up into the sky.
4.   She laughed the milk out of her nose.
5.   The tree grew its branches over the fence.
6.   He wobbled the tray towards the customers.
7.   They bounced the ball across the court.
8.   The sun baked the ground into a hard crust.
9.   The boy whistled the dog into the house.
10. She danced the baby to sleep.
11. He hummed the tune into my ear.
12. He jogged the dog around the park.
13. She tiptoed the glass to the edge of the table.
14. The child skipped the stone across the lake.
15. She twirled the baton in her hand.
16. The fire flickered the shadows across the walls of the cave.
17. The sunbeams danced the shadows on the floor.
18. The sun melted the snow into puddles.
19. The waves crashed the debris onto the shore.
20. The fire crackled the logs in the fireplace.

b. OpenAssistant: Sure, here are twenty examples of intransitive verbs used in caused-motion clauses:
1.   He waved goodbye to his friend.
2.   She wrote a letter to her family.
3.   The dog chased a cat up a tree.
4.   A breeze blew through the leaves.
5.   They pushed the car to the side of the road.
6.   The water flowed downstream.
7.   An earthquake shook the building.
8.   The lightning struck a tree.
9.   The plane took off from the runway.
10. The rain fell from the sky.
11. The sun rose above the horizon.
12. The waves crashed against the shore.
13. The smoke drifted away in the wind.
14. The fireworks exploded high in the air.
15. The bullet pierced through the target.
16. The ball rolled into the hole.
17. The gusts of wind carried the kite away.
18. The water dripped from the faucet.
19. The steam escaped from the boiling pot.
20. The snow fell silently outside my window.

(3) already contains a more challenging prompt. Not only does it ask the model to provide twenty examples of the Caused Motion construction, but it also explicitly requires it to generate examples with intransitive verbs only. Such a prompt, if successful, could, for example, be used to create a list of stimuli sentences for a potential acceptability experiment. In (4a) we can see that ChatGPT does indeed nominate some interesting examples that might be used as stimuli (*She laughed the milk out of her nose*). The output also contains cases where the Caused Motion construction is interpreted as a Resultative (*The sun melted the snow into puddles*), as discussed by Goldberg (2006). At the same time, ChatGPT also provides examples that have the right syntactic form, but not the meaning of the Caused Motion construction: *They paused the game for a bathroom break* exhibits the NP-V-NP-PP structure, but cannot be construed as "They$_1$ caused the-game$_3$ to move towards a-bathroom-break$_4$ by pausing$_2$-ing"). Again, however, OpenAssistant performs considerably worse on this task. Only sentences 3, 5, and 17 are clear instances of the Caused Motion construction. Thirteen examples are in fact instances of the Intransitive Motion construction and do not contain an object. Note that, throughout this Element, we do not ask whether the LLMs will produce *flawless* responses – clearly they do not (yet). Instead, we want to focus on whether those responses can serve as useful *nominations for the linguist's consideration*, and in that respect, (4a) is already impressive, as ChatGPT produces a great number of relevant instances of the argument structure construction under investigation, while OpenAssistant still clearly fails this task. At the same time, these examples also illustrate that the linguist still needs to carefully evaluate the output of conversational AIs in order to distinguish relevant responses from those that are incorrect.

Increasing the complexity of constructions even more, we next asked both generative AIs about the XYZ construction, which, as mentioned in Section 2, requires the blending of several frame input spaces to express a concise, novel idea:

(5)   USER: The XYZ construction, e.g. "Paul (X) is the father (Y) of Sally (Z)" or "Causation (X) is the cement (Y) of the universe (Z)" prompts us to evoke a frame indicated by Y and to blend it with the X-Z information. Please give 10 more examples in which the Y term evokes a conceptual frame to be blended with the X-Z information.

(6)   a. ChatGPT: Sure, here are 10 more examples:·
        1. The internet is the nervous system of modern society.
        2. Gratitude is the memory of the heart.
        3. The library is the brain of the university.
        4. Imagination is the fuel of creativity.

5. Time is the river of life.
6. Music is the medicine of the soul.
7. Language is the bridge between cultures.
8. Curiosity is the compass of exploration.
9. Empathy is the food of human connection.
10. Humor is the band-aid of a stressful day.

b. OpenAssistant: Certainly, here are ten more examples of the XYZ construction:

1. John (X) is the manager (Y) of the team (Z).
2. Success (X) is the result (Y) of hard work (Z).
3. Education (X) is the key (Y) to success (Z).
4. Love (X) is the most powerful (Y) force (Z) in the world.
5. Music (X) is the language (Y) of emotions (Z).
6. Nature (X) is the greatest (Y) artist (Z).
7. Fear (X) is the enemy (Y) of progress (Z).
8. Health (X) is wealth (Y) in disguise (Z).
9. Creativity (X) is the spark (Y) of innovation (Z).
10. Failure (X) is the stepping stone (Y) for achievements (Z).

How creative are the responses that the models give for the XYZ construction? Again, it is unclear which data were in the training sets, but a Google search at least allows for a heuristic assessment of the innovativeness of ChatGPT's example sentences:

(7)   a. The internet is the nervous system of modern society. (4 hits; https://rigf.ru/en/press/?v=archive&id=115&year=2021)
        b. Gratitude is the memory of the heart. (202,000 hits; https://diocesan.com/gratitude-is-the-memory-of-the-heart/)
        c. The library is the brain of the university. (2 hits; http://ublibrary.weebly.com/rules-and-regulations.html)
        d. Imagination is the fuel of creativity. (8 hits; https://anatola.beehiiv.com/p/neuroscience-of-imagination)
        e. Time is the river of life. (492,000 hits; www.goodreads.com/work/quotes/67142076)
        f. Music is the medicine of the soul. (83,100 hits; https://irp.nih.gov/catalyst/27/4/is-music-really-the-medicine-of-the-soul)
        g. Language is the bridge between cultures. (7,890 hits; www.nexus.edu.sg/people/primary-zoe-zhou)
        h. Curiosity is the compass of exploration. (0 hits)
        i. Empathy is the food of human connection. (0 hits)
        j. Humor is the band-aid of a stressful day. (0 hits)

As a Google search (28 March 2023) revealed, (7b, e, f, g) are so frequent that it seems likely that they appeared somewhere in the training data. If so, these would not be creative constructs but only reused, entrenched constructions

(Turner, 2020; Hoffmann, 2022b). Other examples, such as (7a, c, d), do indeed occur on the web, but only very infrequently (with 2 to 8 hits), so for these items, it is next to impossible to assess whether the model simply recombined them or productively constructed them. (7h, i, j) are by far the most interesting instances of the XYZ construction, as these cannot be found on the web (yet). Still, partial matches can nevertheless be found for all three:

(8)   a. **Curiosity is the compass of** the heart and the lust of the mind. (www.andycash.co/dictionary)
      b. As we all know feedback and **empathy is the food of** champions. (https://twitter.com/TemitopeAyodel_/status/1587866741119614976?s=20)
      c. **alcohol is the band-aid of** life (https://twitter.com/animatedtext/status/1094372119448903680?s=20)

OpenAssistant, on the other hand, mostly provides rather uncreative examples, many of which are highly frequent quotes or clichés:

(9)   a. John is the manager of the team. (3 hits; www.espn.com/blog/boston/red-sox/post/_/id/47394/crucible-of-cancer-forges-stronger-bond-between-john-farrell-torey-lovullo)
      b. Success is the result of hard work. (258,000 hits; https://quotefancy.com/quote/916496/Thomas-A-Edison-Success-is-the-result-of-hard-work)
      c. Education is the key to success. (1,170,000 hits; www.intelligenthq.com/why-is-education-the-key-to-success/)
      d. Love is the most powerful force in the world. (64.900 hits; www.goodreads.com/quotes/7364186-love-is-the-most-powerful-force-in-the-world-if).
      e. Music is the language of emotions. (119,000 hits; https://unquote.li/en/quotes/emmanuel-kant/music-is-the-language-of-emotions-a52wxl8wn9)
      f. Nature is the greatest artist. (15,600 hits; https://medium.com/spiritual-tree/an-artist-called-nature-47eb23caf426)
      g. Fear is the enemy of progress. (101,000 hits; https://seekerproject4se.org/2022/08/11/truth-is-the-enemy-of-faith-and-fear-is-the-enemy-of-progress/)
      h. Health is wealth in disguise. (3 hits; www.facebook.com/341405716431476/posts/health-is-wealth-in-disguiseto-mark-todays-world-clean-up-day-toro-youths-have-m/756513928253984/)
      i. Creativity is the spark of innovation. (3,660 hits; www.creativecave.biz/about-us)
      j. Failure is the stepping stone for achievements. (0 hits)

While the full sentence in (9a) is not very frequent, the VP "is the manager of the team" has 2,590,000 hits. Similarly, "wealth in disguise" (9h) and "stepping stone for achievements" (9j) are fairly frequent phrases (with 123,000 and

20,800 hits, respectively). All other examples in (9) can be found several thousand times on the web.

Given that LLMs excel at pattern recognition, it is no surprise that ChatGPT might have encoded chunks such as (8a–c) as highly likely sequences of words, which then leads it to produce novel constructs such as (7h, i, j). After all, (8a–c) already establish a connection between the seemingly independent frames of X and Y in an existing XYZ construct. Are these creative instances of the XYZ construction? As always, a lot depends on one's definition, but these examples at least exhibit a certain degree of novelty and can be considered appropriate uses of the construction, thus meeting two integral properties of standard psychological definitions of creativity (see, e.g., Hoffmann, 2022b). Note that we do not mean to imply that the models are creative or exhibit human behavior. All we want to point out is that they can at least generate products that go beyond their input and are, in this sense, creative. We, thus, want to emphasize the important distinction between creative products and creative producers (Hoffmann, 2022b). To a certain degree, at least, some models, such as ChatGPT, might be able to supply Construction Grammar researchers with (somewhat) creative constructs that can be the starting point for further constructionist analysis (e.g., testing how humans rate the appropriateness of such novel constructs). Other chatty LLMs, such as OpenAssistant, so far, fail to provide particularly interesting novel instances of certain constructional patterns.

Can LLMs also be used to suggest potentially corroborating evidence for constructions? Hoffmann & Bergs (2024) and Hoffmann (unpublished data[7]) argue along these lines, claiming that the pattern-detection functionality of LLMs provides independent support for the claim that speakers possess discourse-level constructions. They illustrate this with *Knock Knock* jokes such as (10) and (11) (source: https://parade.com/944054/parade/knock-knock-jokes/):

(10)   A: Knock, Knock
       B: Who's there?
       A: Luke.
       B: Luke who?
       A: Luke through the peep hole and find out.

(11)   A: Knock, Knock.
       B: Who's there?
       A: Figs.
       B: Figs who?
       A: Figs the doorbell, it's not working!

---

[7] Hoffmann, T. ChatGPT and CxG: The end or future of constructionist research and teaching?

Based on a cursory discussion of the construction in Bergen and Binsted (2015) as well as their introspective analysis, Hoffmann and Bergs (2024) claim that *Knock Knock* jokes are stored as a complex discourse-level construction, with complex FORM–MEANING properties:

(12) FORM: PHONOLOGY: A: /ˈnɒk ˈnɒk/
B: /ˈhuz ðeə/
A: X_1
B: X_1 /ˈhu/
A: Y [contains sth. phonetically similar to X_1]

MORPHOSYNTAX: A: *knock$_V$ knock$_V$*
B: *Who$_{WH}$ is$_{AUX}$ there$_{OBL}$?*
A: X_1
B: X_1 *Who$_{WH}$?*
A: Y

MEANING: SEMANTICS:
PRAGMATICS: function=entertain

As the following example shows, even given a very short prompt, such as in (13), ChatGPT offers support for a constructional analysis of *Knock Knock* jokes and identifies virtually all of the various constructional properties postulated in (12), while OpenAssistant's attempt is less detailed but still suggestive:

(13) USER: Give me a construction grammar analysis of Knock Knock jokes.

(14) a. ChatGPT: Knock Knock jokes are a type of joke that follows a specific construction or formula, which involves a call-and-response format between two speakers. The construction typically follows this format:
Speaker 1: "Knock Knock!"
Speaker 2: "Who's there?"
Speaker 1: [Insert a name or phrase that is a play on words]
Speaker 2: [Repeats the name or phrase]
Speaker 1: [Completes the joke with a punchline that involves a twist or surprise]
This construction involves several linguistic elements that are used in a creative and humorous way to create a joke. The opening phrase "Knock Knock" functions as an attention-getter or signal that a joke is about to be told. The response from Speaker 2, "Who's there?" sets up the joke by inviting Speaker 1 to provide a name or phrase that will be used as the basis for the joke.
        The next element of the construction is the name or phrase that Speaker 1 provides, which is typically a play on words that sets up the punchline of the

joke. This may involve a pun, a homophone, or a double entendre, among other linguistic devices.

The final element of the construction is the punchline, which involves a twist or surprise that plays on the wordplay or pun set up by the name or phrase. The punchline is intended to be unexpected and to create a humorous or absurd effect.

Overall, the construction of Knock Knock jokes involves a combination of linguistic elements, including attention-getters, call-and-response patterns, wordplay, and surprise twists, that are used in a creative and humorous way to create a joke that often relies on the listener's ability to recognize and appreciate the linguistic devices involved.

b. OpenAssistant: Sure, Construction Grammar provides a framework for analyzing how words and phrases are combined into larger structures in natural languages such as English. According to Construction Grammar theory, words and phrases form constructions, which are recurrent patterns of co-occurrences between linguistic elements. These constructions represent stored knowledge about language use and provide speakers with templates for creating new utterances without having to retrieve individual lexemes or word forms one at a time.

Knock knock jokes often follow specific grammatical patterns and constructions. One common type of construction found in Knock knock jokes involves two noun phrases followed by a question word (such as who or what), similar to the following example:

knocker: Who's there?
boo: Boo.
knocker: Boo who?
boo: Don't cry, it's just a joke!

In this structure, the first noun phrase (Who's there?`) functions as the topic of the discourse, while the second noun phrase (Boo) serves as the answer to the question posed in the first element of the construction. This structure creates expectations among listeners about how the exchange will continue and allows them to anticipate potential punchlines based on their familiarity with these patterns. Other types of constructions might involve direct address to interlocutors (e.g., "Oi, you there!"), rhetorical questions (e.g., Why did the tomato turn red? Because it saw the salad dressing), or elliptical expressions ("You know … right? Or was it left?").

Finally, AI LLM chatbots can nominate items for the linguist to consider as supporting evidence for existing constructions, and in general propose items worth exploring. For example, the linguist might ask the chatbot to propose other discourse-level constructions:

(15)   USER: Name ten other discourse-level patterns that can be analyzed as constructions.

(16)   a. ChatGPT: Sure, here are ten more examples of discourse-level patterns that can be analyzed as constructions:

Apology Construction: This construction typically begins with an expression of regret, followed by an acknowledgement of fault or responsibility, and ends with a request for forgiveness or a promise to make amends.

Job Interview Construction: This construction typically begins with an introduction of the candidate, followed by a discussion of their qualifications and experience, and ends with a question and answer period.

Debate Construction: This construction typically begins with an introduction of the topic and the speakers, followed by a presentation of arguments and counterarguments, and ends with a conclusion or resolution.

News Report Construction: This construction typically begins with a headline or lead-in, followed by a presentation of facts and details, and ends with a conclusion or summary.

Wedding Toast Construction: This construction typically begins with an expression of congratulations or best wishes, followed by anecdotes and memories of the couple, and ends with a toast to their future together.

Political Speech Construction: This construction typically begins with an introduction of the speaker and the topic, followed by a presentation of their platform and policy proposals, and ends with a call to action or a message of hope.

Eulogy Construction: This construction typically begins with an expression of condolences, followed by memories and stories of the deceased, and ends with a message of comfort and closure.

Sermon Construction: This construction typically begins with a scripture or reading, followed by a presentation of the message or lesson, and ends with a call to action or a message of inspiration.

Stand-up Comedy Construction: This construction typically begins with a setup or premise, followed by a punchline or joke, and ends with a tagline or callback.

Podcast Interview Construction: This construction typically begins with an introduction of the guest and the topic, followed by a discussion of their background and expertise, and ends with a Q&A session or a call to action.

b. OpenAssistant: Here are ten other discourse level patterns that could be analyzed using construction grammer
Exclamative sentences/constructions
Rhetorical questions
Advice seeking/requesting
Politeness strategies
Complaining
Agreeing/disagreenging
Reason giving/arguing
Condolancing
Aggressiveness·
Threats

Notice that ChatGPT responds with analyses, but OpenAssistant sticks to the minimum and supplies only the labels. Such performance can be controlled by engineering a different prompt. We do not dive into the possibilities of alternative prompting here.

The above text types, obviously, vary considerably in their generality, and construction grammarians will have to investigate carefully whether there is any cognitive evidence that these discourse patterns are stored as constructions. Nevertheless, as a first step, it is also possible to query models for further details that might support such an analysis. (17–18) illustrates this for prototypical apologies:

(17)   USER: Give a detailed analysis of FORM and MEANING elements of the Apology Construction.

(18)   a. ChatGPT: The Apology Construction is a discourse-level pattern that speakers use when they want to express regret, remorse, or sorrow for something that they have done or failed to do. It typically involves a specific structure and a set of linguistic markers that indicate the speaker's attitude towards the situation.
FORM:
The Apology Construction has a specific form that includes the following elements:
Expression of regret or remorse: This is usually the first element of the Apology Construction and is often signaled by an apology formula, such as "I'm sorry" or "I apologize".
Acknowledgment of responsibility: The speaker takes responsibility for the action or situation that caused the harm, often using verbs like "I did" or "I failed to".
Explanation or justification (optional): The speaker may provide an explanation or justification for their behavior, but this is not always necessary.
Promise of repair or restitution: The speaker offers to make things right, often by offering to do something to fix the situation or prevent it from happening again.
MEANING:
The Apology Construction is used to convey a range of meanings, including:
Regret or remorse: The Apology Construction is primarily used to express feelings of regret or remorse for something that the speaker has done or failed to do. The expression of regret or remorse is a way for the speaker to acknowledge the harm that has been caused and to show that they understand the impact of their actions.
Responsibility: The Apology Construction is also used to acknowledge responsibility for the situation or action that caused harm. This is an important part of the apology because it shows that the speaker is willing to take ownership of their actions and to accept the consequences.

Repair or restitution: The Apology Construction often includes a promise of repair or restitution, which is a way for the speaker to demonstrate their commitment to making things right. This can involve a specific action or set of actions that the speaker will take to repair the harm caused or prevent it from happening again.

Respect: The Apology Construction is also used to show respect for the person or people who have been harmed. By acknowledging the harm that has been caused and taking responsibility for it, the speaker is demonstrating their respect for the feelings and experiences of others.

In summary, the Apology Construction is a discourse-level pattern that speakers use to express regret, remorse, or sorrow for something that they have done or failed to do. The construction has a specific form that includes an expression of regret or remorse, an acknowledgment of responsibility, an explanation or justification (optional), and a promise of repair or restitution. The construction is used to convey meanings such as regret or remorse, responsibility, repair or restitution, and respect.

b. OpenAssistant: The Apology Construction involves two main components – FORM and MEANING. Let's take a closer look at both elements.

FORM: The Apology Construction consists of four key parts: a) Acknowledgment: This component signals the beginning of the apology, acknowledging that some wrongdoing occurred. For example: "I'm sorry for what happened . . . " b) Expression of regret: Expressions of regret convey remorseful feelings, and acknowledge responsibility for one's actions. For example: "I feel really bad about it." c) Offer of repair: This part offers restitution or reparation, indicating steps taken to prevent similar situations from happening again. For example: "I'll make sure it doesn't happen again." d) Closure statement: The last part finalizes the apology by saying "thank you," or something similar, signaling the end of the apology. For example: "Thanks for listening."

MEANING: The Meaning of the Apology Construction conveys repentance for past behaviors. It expresses empathy and understanding toward others, as well as respect for social norms. By offering an apology, speakers demonstrate their willingness to fix things and restore relationships, which helps build trust and strengthen bonds between people.

Apologies come in various shapes and forms and have been the subject of numerous linguistic studies (cf., e.g. Leech, 2014: 115–133). Similarly, tons of websites (e.g., https://ggia.berkeley.edu/practice/making_an_effective_apology) offer advice as to how one should apologize. We do not know whether our chosen LLMs had access to any of those sources. Nevertheless, what they do offer the linguist are schematic form–meaning representations such as (18a and b) that could be used as a starting point for the investigation of an Apology construction. The AI LLM chatbots can then be asked further to compose an appropriate construct using the Apology construction:

(19)   USER: Give me an example of a full text that is created by the Apology
         Construction. Indicate which parts correspond to which FORM or MEANING
         component of the construction.

(20)   a. ChatGPT: Here is an example of a full text that follows the Apology
         Construction:
         FORM:
         Attention-getter
         Expression of regret
         Explanation of what went wrong
         Acknowledgment of responsibility
         Declaration of repentance
         Offer of repair
         Request for forgiveness
         Closing
         MEANING:
         The Apology Construction is used to express remorse and seek forgiveness
         after a wrong has been committed. The speaker must show that they under-
         stand what they did wrong and take responsibility for their actions. They must
         also demonstrate a sincere desire to make things right and offer a plan for how
         they can do so. Finally, the speaker must ask for forgiveness and offer a closing
         that shows their commitment to making things right.
         Here's an example text that follows the Apology Construction:
         FORM:
         Attention-getter: "I want to start by saying how sorry I am."
         Expression of regret: "I regret my actions and the hurt that I have caused."
         Explanation of what went wrong: "I was not thinking clearly and acted
         impulsively."
         Acknowledgment of responsibility: "I take full responsibility for my actions
         and the consequences that have resulted."
         Declaration of repentance: "I understand how my actions have affected you
         and I am committed to making things right."
         Offer of repair: "I would like to offer to pay for any damages and work to
         repair our relationship."
         Request for forgiveness: "I hope you can find it in your heart to forgive me."
         Closing: "I want you to know that I value our relationship and will do
         everything in my power to make things right."
         MEANING:
         The speaker is expressing remorse and taking responsibility for their
         actions. They understand that their actions have caused harm and are
         committed to repairing the damage and making things right. The speaker
         is seeking forgiveness and demonstrating a genuine desire to repair the
         relationship.

         b. OpenAssistant:
         Example: "I would like to apologize for my behavior yesterday during our
         meeting. I realize now how inconsiderate I was acting when interrupting you,

not letting you finish speaking. It was unprofessional and unethical on my behalf, and I understand the frustration that caused in our team. Moreover, my attitude may have undermined your credibility with your higher ups, who were also present. From this point forward, I will work hard to ensure that our communication is more balanced by asking thoughtful questions instead of immediately sharing my opinions, so we can have constructive dialogue without interruption. Once again, I apologize deeply for my misbehavior".

Both responses offer a suitable construct, but ChatGPT conforms to the prompt for an analysis, while OpenAssistant does not. The suggested constructs in (20) sound formulaic (cf., e.g. "I regret my actions and the hurt that I have caused." or "I would like to offer to pay for any damages and work to repair our relationship."). Still, both models offer suitable constructs, and ChatGPT seems to have also identified a general template (an authentic and potentially successful human apology will, obviously, have to be more personal and make more concrete references to the situation for which the speaker is apologizing). More interesting, from a theoretical point of view, is the fact that the constructional properties of (18a) and (20a) are not identical. (20a) adds certain elements (such as the Attention-getter or the Explanation of what went wrong slot). Since the content of the previous discourse seems to be important for the answers a model provides, it is perhaps important to note that, in the case of ChatGPT but not OpenAssistant, in-between (17) and (19), we first issued the following two prompts, (21) and (22), having to do with the Wedding Toast construction:

(21)   USER: Give a detailed analysis of FORM and MEANING elements of the Wedding Toast Construction.

(22)   a. ChatGPT: The Wedding Toast Construction is a discourse-level pattern that typically occurs in the context of a wedding reception or ceremony, where a speaker offers a speech or toast to honor and congratulate the newlyweds.
FORM:
The Wedding Toast Construction typically includes the following form elements:
Address: The speaker begins by addressing the audience and acknowledging their presence.
Example: "Ladies and gentlemen, distinguished guests, friends and family of the bride and groom ... "
Congratulations: The speaker congratulates the newlyweds on their marriage and wishes them a happy future together.
Example: "I want to start by congratulating [Bride's name] and [Groom's name] on their wedding day. May your future be filled with love, laughter, and joy."

Personal anecdotes: The speaker may share personal stories or anecdotes about the newlyweds or their relationship to add a personal touch to the speech.

Example: "I remember when [Bride's name] first told me about [Groom's name], and how she knew he was the one for her. Seeing them together today, I know she was right."

Advice: The speaker may offer advice to the newlyweds on how to have a successful and happy marriage.

Example: "Marriage is not always easy, but it is worth it. My advice to you both is to communicate openly, cherish each other, and never forget the love that brought you together today."

Toast: The speaker raises a glass to the newlyweds and invites the audience to join in a toast to their happiness.

Example: "So let us raise a glass to [Bride's name] and [Groom's name], and wish them all the happiness in the world!"

MEANING:

The Wedding Toast Construction serves a social function in celebrating and honoring the newlyweds' union, as well as providing guidance and support for their future together. The speech typically expresses feelings of happiness, love, and goodwill towards the newlyweds, and may include humorous or sentimental anecdotes to add a personal touch. The advice offered in the speech serves to provide guidance and support for the couple as they embark on their new life together. The toast to the newlyweds is a symbolic gesture of wishing them all the best for their future together.

b. OpenAssistant: Certainly!

Form: The Wedding Toast Construction typically follows a specific form that includes several stages or sections. These include:

Opening remarks: The speaker begins by introducing themselves and explaining their connection to the couple being honored. They might share memories or stories about how they met, or simply offer warm wishes and best regards.

Contextualization: Next, the speaker provides relevant background information about the couple or event itself. This may include details about their courtship, engagement story, special moments shared together, etc.

Compliments: During this stage, the speaker extends formal or informal expressions of admiration, praise, gratitude, love, affection, respect, appreciation, esteem, pride, satisfaction, joy, happiness, support or approval regarding one or both members of the newlywed pair. Their words aim to celebrate their union, and inspire guests to raise glasses and join in the festivities.

Well-Wishes / Blessings: The next portion of the speech centers around hopeful expectations, sentiments, good intentions, desires, aspirations, prayer requests, vibes, energy, prayers, benedictions, supplications, petitions, appeals, blessings, curses, exhortations, encouragements, recommendations, or entreaties for happiness, success, fulfillment, longevity, prosperity, wealth, health, fertility, harmony, bliss, peace, love or companionship for the couple.

Again, we do not know the data on which the model has been trained. The data might include substantial examples of wedding toasts. In any event, it is clear that the chatty model can respond to local context as provided in its chat history to produce a constructional analysis of the text type.

As before, we asked both LLMs to provide us with an example of this discourse-level construction:

(23) USER: Give me an example of a full text that is created by the Wedding Toast Construction. Indicate which parts correspond to which FORM or MEANING component of the construction.

(24) a. ChatGPT: Certainly, here's an example of a text that follows the Wedding Toast Construction:
FORM:
Address the audience
Express gratitude to hosts and guests
Recall personal anecdote about the couple
Offer congratulations and well-wishes
Raise a toast to the newlyweds
MEANING:
This construction is used in a wedding setting to honor and congratulate the newlyweds, while also expressing gratitude to the hosts and guests. The personal anecdote provides a heartfelt and intimate touch to the speech, while the toast at the end celebrates the couple's union.
Example Text:
Good evening everyone,
First of all, I would like to thank [HOST NAME] for hosting such a beautiful wedding and gathering us all here tonight to celebrate the marriage of [BRIDE NAME] and [GROOM NAME]. It's an honor to be part of this special occasion.
[PERSONAL ANECDOTE: Insert a personal anecdote about the couple, such as how they met, a funny story about their relationship, or a touching moment you shared with them.]
I want to congratulate you both on finding each other and building such a strong and loving relationship. [BRIDE NAME], you look absolutely stunning today, and [GROOM NAME], you are one lucky man.
May your marriage be filled with love, happiness, and laughter. [INSERT WELL-WISHES OR ADVICE, IF DESIRED.] Let's raise a glass to the newlyweds – cheers!
[RAISE A TOAST TO THE NEWLYWEDS: Insert a toast to the couple, such as "To [BRIDE NAME] and [GROOM NAME], may your love continue to grow stronger with each passing day."]
Thank you and enjoy the rest of the evening.

b. OpenAssistant: Certainly!
Form: The Wedding Toast Construction typically follows a specific form that includes several stages or sections. These include:
Opening remarks: The speaker begins by introducing themselves and explaining their connection to the couple being honored. They might share memories or stories about how they met, or simply offer warm wishes and best regards.
Contextualization: Next, the speaker provides relevant background information about the couple or event itself. This may include details about their courtship, engagement story, special moments shared together, etc.
Compliments: During this stage, the speaker extends formal or informal expressions of admiration, praise, gratitude, love, affection, respect, appreciation, esteem, pride, satisfaction, joy, happiness, support or approval regarding one or both members of the newlywed pair. Their words aim to celebrate their union, and inspire guests to raise glasses and join in the festivities.
Well-Wishes / Blessings: The next portion of the speech centers around hopeful expectations, sentiments, good intentions, desires, aspirations, prayer requests, vibes, energy, prayers, benedictions, supplications, petitions, appeals, blessings, curses, exhortations, encouragements, recommendations, or entreaties for happiness, success, fulfillment, longevity, prosperity, wealth, health, fertility, harmony, bliss, peace, love or companionship for the couple.

Again, we find slight differences between the constructional templates proposed by ChatGPT in (22a) and (24a) for which we currently have no explanation: Congratulations appear in a different place on the FORM pole (no. 4 in (24a) instead of no. 2 in (22a)) and Advice is only mentioned in passing in (24a) in the suggested exemplar of the construction "[INSERT WELL-WISHES OR ADVICE, IF DESIRED]", but not on the FORM pole. OpenAssistant, by contrast, offers the same general template in both 21b and 23b: Form: Opening remarks, Contextualization, Compliments, Well-Wishes / Blessings.

These differences, however, are minor, if worth exploring. We believe that the above examples nevertheless indicate that conversational LLMs such as ChatGPT and OpenAssistant are already helpful tools for investigating discourse-level constructions.

At this point, let us take a moment to dive deeper into the limitations of AI LLM chatbots when used for supporting construction grammarians in their analyses.

4 Limitations of LLMs for Constructional Analysis

On top of the limitations already pointed out in the chat sequences in the previous section, the tests we conducted with ChatGPT and OpenAssistant reveal two major challenges for the use of an AI LLM chatbot as a tool for constructionist analyses: multilinguality and semantics. In this section, we look into them in more detail.

4.1 Constructions in Languages Other Than English

As shown in the previous section, more precisely in (3 and 4), both AI LLM chatbots proposed a list of twenty examples of a caused motion clause with an intransitive verb. Some were actually instances of the Resultative construction, some verbs were not intransitive, yet many could be regarded as possible instances of the Caused Motion construction. During our tests with the chatbots, we also prompted them to analyze constructions in other languages. In the remainder of this section, we discuss two of the prompts we provided to both AI LLM chatbots and their responses to them.

The first prompt concerns the Split Argument construction in Brazilian Portuguese. Such a construction conforms to the NP V NP syntactic pattern – the same pattern present in the Active Transitive construction – but instead of featuring an agentive subject NP and a patient-like object NP, it assigns a patient reading to both NPs, evoking the Undergoing frame (Almeida, 2016, 2022; Matos et al., 2017). There are four types of the Split Argument construction: Artifact, Body part, Possession, and Entity-attribute (Sampaio, 2010), exemplified in (25–28).

(25)　　O celular　　　quebrou　　　　a tela.
　　　　The cell phone　break.PST.3SG　the screen
　　　　The screen in my cell phone cracked.

(26)　　O bebê　　　quebrou　　　　o braço.
　　　　The baby　　break.PST.3SG　the arm
　　　　The baby broke his arm.

(27)　　Eu　　furei　　　　　o pneu.
　　　　I　　pierce.PST.1SG　the tire
　　　　I got a flat tire.

(28)　　A gasolina　　　subiu　　　　　o preço.
　　　　The gasoline　　go-up.PST.3SG　the price
　　　　Gas prices went up.

Note that, in all four of them, some sort of semantic relationship holds between the element in the first NP slot and the NP in the second: whole–part, body–body part, possessor–possession, or entity–attribute. In this construction, the composition of the two NPs undergoes some sort of change and the fact that the semantic argument of Undergoing is split into two parts profiles the element in the first NP slot (Sampaio, 2010).

We used the first subtype of the Split Argument construction to prompt the chatbots, as shown in (29–32), where sentences in Portuguese have been glossed by us for the sake of comprehension. OpenAssistant already provided a translation into English for each sentence in Brazilian Portuguese. For the sake of better visualization, those translations were moved to the last line of each example, following the translation provided by us. The chat sequence demonstrates that neither chatbot provides, in its first attempt, one single correct example for the Split Argument construction. When corrected by the user, they once again failed in the task: In (32), for ChatGPT, only sentence 6 and (with some contextualization effort) sentence 5 can be regarded as instances of the Split Argument construction. Although in some cases ChatGPT chooses nonhuman and nonanimate subjects for the sentences it creates – a feature common in the Split Argument construction with artifacts – when it does so, it usually comes up with sentences where the first NP gains an instrumental reading. For OpenAssistant, once again, none of the sentences are instances of the construction. OpenAssistant also performs worse in regard to the grammaticality of the sentences in Brazilian Portuguese, and even makes mistakes when proposing instances of the Transitive construction. Some sentences lack fluency or sound odd. There are also some subword-level issues, such as the word *demolidaram* in the last sentence produced by OpenAssistant, after the correction. The verb in Portuguese would be *demoliram*.

(29)   USER: Brazilian Portuguese has two constructions sharing the same formal pattern, namely one involving a noun phrase, a verb phrase and another noun phrase. One of those constructions is the Active transitive construction, where the first noun phrase is an agent who acts on the patient expressed in the second noun phrase. An example of such a construction would be the sentence "A cozinheira quebrou as nozes". The other construction is the Split argument construction, where both noun phrases are a patient for the action expressed in the verb. Usually, there is a whole-part relation between the first noun phrase and the second one. An example of such a construction is the sentence "A panela quebrou o cabo". Please give me ten additional examples for each type of constructions mentioned above. Make sure not to repeat the verbs in the example lists.

(30)   a. ChatGPT:
       Active transitive construction:
       1. O menino   jogou   a bola.
           The boy   throw.PST.3SG   the ball
           The boy threw the ball.
       2. O gato   arranhou   a cadeira.
           The cat   scratch.PST.3SG   the chair
           The cat scratched the chair.

3.	O pintor	pintou	a parede.
	The painter	paint.PST.3SG	the wall
	The painter painted the wall.		
4.	O motorista	dirigiu	o carro.
	The driver	drive.PST.3SG	the car
	The driver drove the car.		
5.	O médico	examinou	o paciente.
	The doctor	examine.PST.3SG	the patient
	The doctor examined the patient.		
6.	O garçom	serviu	o prato.
	The waiter	serve.PST.3SG	the dish
	The waiter served the dish.		
7.	O bombeiro	apagou	o fogo.
	The firefighter	put out.PST.3SG	the fire
	The firefighter put out the fire.		
8.	A professora	corrigiu	a prova.
	The teacher	grade.PST.3SG	the test
	The teacher graded the test.		
9.	O pedreiro	construiu	a casa.
	The mason	build.PST.3SG	the house
	The mason built the house.		
10.	O jardineiro	plantou	as flores.
	The gardener	plant.PST.3SG	the flowers
	The gardener planted the flowers.		

Split argument construction:

1.	O cão	comeu	o osso.
	The dog	eat.PST.3SG	the bone
	The dog ate the bone.		
2.	O martelo	quebrou	a pedra.
	The hammer	break.PST.3SG	the stone
	The hammer broke the stone.		
3.	O fogo	queimou	a madeira.
	The fire	burn.PST.3SG	the wood
	The fire burnt the wood.		
4.	A faca	cortou	a carne.
	The knife	cut.PST.3SG	the meat
	The knife cut the meat.		
5.	A tesoura	rasgou	o papel.
	The scissors	tear.PST.3SG	the paper
	The scissors tore the paper.		
6.	A chave	abriu	a porta.
	The key	open.PST.3SG	the door
	The key opened the door.		
7.	O sal	danificou	o carro.
	The salt	damage.PST.3SG	the car
	The salt damaged the car.		

8. A tempestade   arrancou   a árvore.
    The storm   rip out.PST.3SG   the tree
    The storm uprooted the tree.
9. O tempo   desgastou   o metal.
    The time   wear out.PST.3SG the metal
    The weather corroded the metal.
10. O sol   derreteu   o gelo.
    The sun   melt.PST.3SG   the ice
    The sun melted the ice.

b. OpenAssistant: Sure, here are some more examples of the active transitive construction:

Active Transitive Construction:

1. * O garoto jogador de futebol   atirou   em um pênalti.
    The boy player of soccer   shoot.PST.3SG   in a penalty
    * *The boy fired at a penalty.*
    (The boy soccer player took a penalty kick.)
2. A professora   ensinou   os alunos   como
    The teacher   teach.PST.3SG   the students how
    resolver   equações.
    solve.INF   equations
    The teacher taught the students how to solve equations.
    (The teacher taught the students how to solve equations.)
3. Os bombeiros   apagaram   o fogo na casa.
    The firefighters   put out.PST.3SG   the fire in the house
    The firefighters put out the fire in the house.
    (The firefighters put out the fire in the house.)
4. O motorista   dirigiu   o carro até a estação de trem.
    The driver   drive.PST.3SG   the car to the station of train
    The driver drove the car to the train station.
    (The driver drove the car to the train station.)
5. Os pescadores   capturam   peixes com redes e armadilhas.
    The fisherman   capture.PRES.3SG   fishes with nets and traps
    Fishermen catch fish with nets and traps.
    (Fishermen catch fish with nets and traps.)
6. A enfermeira   administrou   uma vacina à criança.
    The nurse   administer.PST.3SG a vaccine to the child
    The nurse administered a vaccine to the child.
    (The nurse administered a vaccine to the child.)
7. Os construtores   estão   reconstruindo a ponte
    The builders   be.PRES.3PL   rebuild.GER   the bridge
    sobre o rio.
    over the river
    The builders are rebuilding the bridge over the river.
    (The builders are rebuilding the bridge over the river.)

8. A bibliotecária ajudou o estudante a encontrar
The librarian help.PST.3SG the student to find.INF
livros relevantes para seu trabalho.
books relevant for his work
The librarian helped the student find books relevant to his work
(The librarian helped the student find relevant books for their work.)

9. * O técnico fixou o computador danificado durante
The technician fixate.PST.3SG the computer damaged during
a noite.
the night
* *The technician fixated the damaged computer during the night.*
(The technician repaired the broken computer during the night.)

10. O arquiteto projetou um novo prédio moderno e
The architect project.PST.3SG a new building modern and
elegante.
elegant.
The architect designed a new modern and elegant building.
(The architect designed a new modern and elegant building.)

And here are some examples of the split argument construction:
Split Argument Construction:

1. ? As poltronas de couro estragadas podem ser
The armchairs of leather damaged can.PRES.3PL be.inf
consertadas por um tapete de mesa.
fix.PART by a rug of table
? The damaged leather armchairs can be fixed using a placemat.
(Torn leather chairs can be fixed by a placemat)

2. Os dentes do meu filho se romperam devido ao
The teeth of the my son self break.PST.3SG due to the
suco natural de uva.
juice natural of grape
My son's teeth broke due to natural grape juice.
(My son's teeth broke due to grape juice).

3. Deve- se abster deste vinho, pois
must.PRES.3SG self avoid.INF of this wine because
contém álcool.
contain.PRES.3SG alcohol
One should avoid this wine because it contains alcohol
(You should stay away from this wine because it contains alcohol)

4. * Desculpa- te comigo, esqueci
apologize.IMP.2SG you.OBL with me forget.PST.1SG
minha bolsa nas traseiras da táxi.
my purse in the backs of the taxi.
* *Apologize to me because I forgot my purse in the backs of your taxi.*
(I'm sorry I forget my purse inside your taxi)

(31)   USER: The examples created for the Split argument construction are
        wrong. Note that in "A panela quebrou o cabo", the noun phrase "o
        cabo" represents a part of the object indicated by the noun phrase "a
        panela". Another good example of the Split argument construction would
        be "A menina quebrou o braço", meaning that the action was not per-
        formed on purpose, but that the entity represented by "a menina" suffered
        the event in the verb "quebrou".

(32)   a. ChatGPT: Thank you for bringing this to my attention. I apologize for the
        mistake. Here are ten additional examples for the Split argument construction
        that correctly demonstrate the whole-part relationship between the first
        and second noun phrases:

        1.   O aluno   rasgou   a folha do caderno.
             The student   tear.PST.3SG   the page of the notebook
             The student tore the notebook page.

        2.   O vento   derrubou   a árvore.
             The wind   overturn.PST.3SG the tree
             The wind uprooted the tree.

        3.   A criança   partiu   o brinquedo.
             The child   split.PST.3SG   the toy
             The child broke the toy.

        4.   O cachorro   mastigou   o sapato.
             The dog   chew.PST.3SG   the shoe
             The dog chewed the shoe.

        5.   O caminhão   esmagou   o vidro.
             The truck   crashed.PST.3SG   the glass
             The truck's windshield crashed.

        6.   O jogador   rompeu   o ligamento.
             The player   break.PST.3SG   the ligament
             The player tore the ligament.

        7.   O garçom   derrubou   a bandeja.
             The waiter   drop.PST.3SG   the tray
             The waiter dropped the tray.

        8.   A tesoura   quebrou   a ponta do lápis.
             The scissors   break.PST.3SG   the tip of the pencil
             The scissors broke the tip of the pencil.

        9.   O bêbado   quebrou   a garrafa.
             The drunk   break.PST.3SG   the bottle
             The drunk person broke the bottle.

        10. O carro   atropelou   o pedestre.
             The car   run over.PST.3SG the pedestrian
             The car ran over the pedestrian.

        b. OpenAssistant: You are correct, I apologize for the confusion. Thank you
        for bringing it to my attention! Here are some corrected examples for the split
        argument construction in Brazilian Portuguese:

1.   O pai   cortou   o cabelo do filho.
        The father   cut.PST.3SG   the hair of the son
        The father cut his son's hair.
        (The father cut his son's hair.)

2.   O médico   removeu   o apêndice do paciente.
        The doctor   remove.PST.3SG   the appendix of the patient
        The doctor removed the appendix from the patient.
        (The doctor removed the appendix from the patient.)

3.   A professora   marcou   o papel do aluno.
        The teacher   mark.PST.3SG   the paper of the student
        The teacher put a mark on the student's paper.
        (The teacher marked up the paper of the student.)

4.   A governanta   varreu   o quarto da princesa.
        The governess   sweep.PST.3SG   the room of the princess
        The governess swept the princess' room.
        (The governess swept the princess' room.)

5.   * O robô   limpou   a sujeira das lavastoves.
        The robot   clean.PST.3SG   the dirt of the NON-WORD
        * *The robot cleaned the dirt of the ???.*
        (The robot cleaned the dirt from the dishwashers.)

6.   O padeiro   levou   o pão   caseiro
        The baker   take.PST.3SG   the bread   home-made
        ao mercado.
        to the market
        The baker took homemade bread to market.
        (The baker took homemade bread to market.)

7.   O carpinteiro   pintou   a mesa com verniz fosco.
        The carpenter   paint.PST.3SG   the table with varnish matte
        The carpenter painted the table with matte varnish.
        (The carpenter painted the table with flat enamel paint.)

8.   A namorada   comprou   flores para o boyfriend.
        The girlfriend   buy.PST.3SG   flowers for the boyfriend
        The girlfriend bought flowers for her boyfriend.
        (The girlfriend bought flowers for her boyfriend.)

9.   Os bandidos   roubaram   o dinheiro dos bancos.
        The criminals   rob.PST.3SG   the money of the banks
        The criminals robbed the money from the banks
        (The robbers stole money from banks.)

10. * Os operários   demolidaram   o edifício
        The workers   NON-WORD.PST.3PL   the building
        com explosivos.
        with explosives
        * *The workers ??? the building with explosives.*
        (The workers demolished the building with explosives.)

4.2 Constructional Semantics

When formulating analyses of the semantics of constructions, AI LLM chatbots may get confused. To further clarify such a limitation, we prompted the models with the x-safe N construction discussed in Fauconnier and Turner (2002). The resulting dialogue is shown in (33–36).

(33)   USER: Provide the construction grammar analysis of the construction licensing expressions such as "shark-safe beach", "child-safe beach" and "tsunami-safe beach". Explain the form and meaning properties of this construction.

(34)   a. ChatGPT: The construction "X-safe Y" is a nominal compound construction that is commonly used to describe a particular characteristic of the Y (the noun being modified) in relation to the potential danger of X (the modifying noun). For example, "shark-safe beach" means a beach where people are safe from sharks. Similarly, "child-safe beach" refers to a beach that is safe for children, and "tsunami-safe beach" is a beach that is safe from tsunamis. Construction Grammar provides a framework for analyzing such constructions by identifying their form and meaning properties. In this case, the construction "X-safe Y" can be analyzed as follows:

Form:

The construction consists of two nouns in a compound structure.

The first noun (X) modifies the second noun (Y).

The modifier "safe" is a morpheme that signals the relationship between X and Y.

Meaning:

The construction conveys the idea that Y is protected from the potential danger posed by X.

The meaning of the construction is compositional, in that the meaning of "safe" is derived from its component parts: "free from harm or danger."

The construction is context-dependent, in that the type of danger implied by X depends on the knowledge and experience of the speaker and the listener.

In summary, the "X-safe Y" construction is a type of nominal compound that conveys the meaning that Y is protected from the potential danger posed by X. Its form consists of two nouns in a compound structure, with the first noun modifying the second noun, and the modifier "safe" indicating the relationship between X and Y. Its meaning is compositional and context-dependent.

b. OpenAssistant:

This is an interesting feature in English whereby adjectives precede head nouns and their combination can act as modifiers or licenses for other related words. In the cases provided, we have:

shark-safe: Safe from sharks attack. Typically used at beaches which are considered protected from shark attacks.

Meaning: Shark free area near water, usually applies for swimming areas.

child-safe: Protected from children injury or harmful actions done by them. It typically applied in homes when parents want to keep dangerous stuff away from kids reach. tsunami-safe: Secured from Tsunami. Means that the region will stay safe during natural disaster events like earth quakes triggered waves floods.

By providing additional details, this feature gives context and clarifies information about certain places, objects, conditions, etc., making language usage easier, specific and richer.

(35) USER: There is a contradiction in your analysis. You say that the X position conveys a potential danger. But you also say that children in "child-safe beach" are protected from a danger. Which is the correct analysis?

(36) a. ChatGPT:

Thank you for pointing that out. I apologize for the confusion in my previous response.

Upon further reflection, it is more accurate to say that the "X-safe Y" construction conveys the idea that Y is protected from the potential harm or negative effects that may be caused by X. In the case of "child-safe beach," the potential harm or negative effect that the construction is conveying protection from is not necessarily an inherent danger of children themselves, but rather hazards or risks that may be present on a beach that could harm children. Therefore, in the "child-safe beach" construction, the noun "child" does not necessarily convey the potential danger, but rather the population for whom the safety is being ensured. The modifier "safe" signals the relationship between "child" and "beach," conveying the idea that the beach is safe for children to play on without being harmed or exposed to danger or risks.

I hope this clarification resolves the contradiction and provides a clearer understanding of the "X-safe Y" construction.

b. OpenAssistant: My apologies for any confusion caused by my previous answer. You are right; there is indeed a contradictory statement in my reply regarding the use of the word "children-safe" implying safety rather than danger. Let me revise it here under:

The construction of licensing expressions involve the modification of main word elements by qualifying attributes expressed through relative clauses introduced by appropriate prepositions. Some examples include:

"shark-free" – meaning a place without sharks, indicating safety

"children proof" – denoting something difficult or impossible for children to damage

And finally, the "tsunami-proof/resistant" implies structural strength against large scale wave surges

The x-safe N construction is a good example of how more schematic constructions may play a key role in meaning production when interacting with lexical items. The adjective *safe*, as pointed out in footnote 1, may evoke both the `Being_at_risk` and the `Risky_situation` frames. In the examples in the prompt, it evokes the former, which comprises three core elements: the **Asset** that should be protected from the risk, and either a **Dangerous_entity** or a **Harmful_event** threatening the **Asset**. The most interesting aspect of the x-safe N construction is that the x slot may be filled by lexical items instantiating any of the three elements of the `Being_at_risk` frame. The correct interpretation and mental labeling of the noun in the x slot by the speaker derives from the calculation of which would be the most likely framing of x in the `Being_at_risk` frame, given the semantics of the noun modified by *safe.a*.

Both chatbots struggle with interpretation and provide confusing and contradictory explanations for the semantics of this construction, even when informed of their mistakes. Research on probing LLMs for their ability to represent form and meaning information about constructions (Weissweiler et al., 2022) indicates that the semantic pole of constructions is more challenging for such models. This example, in correlation with the analysis provided for the *un*-V construction, raises the question of whether the architecture of LLMs negatively influences their potential to serve as copilots for linguists. Linguistic analysis is, of course, about finding patterns. Nonetheless, language does not abide by absolute, compositional patterns, as constructionist analyses have been demonstrating since the 1980s. While the AI LLM chatbot can often help the linguist, it can often fail the linguist. Using the chatbot requires the linguist to be vigilant and to decide what counts as help and what counts as error. The linguist must always keep the copilot out of the pilot's seat. Needless to say, this condition of chatbots based on LLMs imposes comprehensive responsibility and labor on the linguist to evaluate the output and prompt the chatbot to improve.

We now turn to a more detailed investigation of how AI LLM chatbots behave in experiments for building semantic analysis based on Frame Semantics.

5 Cognitive Frames and FrameNet

Our principal illustration of the possibility of using AI as a copilot for research in Construction Grammar is the use of an AI LLM chatbot as a copilot for doing Frame Semantics. Words – or more precisely, lexical units – often prompt for frames. In fact, Diessel (2019) has recently argued that the meaning pole of lexical units is the access point to the rich encyclopedic frames that make up our mental network of meaning. We also want to focus on frames because (1) Frame Semantics is a principal part of CxG; and (2) there already exists a major, global computational lexicographic research project, FrameNet, for capturing and analyzing these lexical constructions. Accordingly, we are in a position to run experiments in which the performance of AI LLM chatbots is measured against the existing FrameNet analyses and coverage. We have done just that and present the results in the next section.

Creating an entry for FrameNet is extraordinarily laborious. Although more than a thousand cognitive frames – and the lexical units evoking them – have been characterized in FrameNet, very many more need to be built. Tools have been built to help this project, such as Lutma – "a collaborative, semi-constrained, tutorial-based tool for contributing frames and lexical units to the Global FrameNet initiative" (Torrent et al., 2022: 100). Can an AI LLM chatbot assist the researcher who is attempting to expand FrameNet? Can it assist the user of Lutma?

In this section, we present routines for prompting AI chatbots to assist linguists in frame building. We also analyze the limitations of the chatbots and some of their potential risks. Results indicate that the two chatbots evaluated in this Element can propose structures similar to frames and frame elements; propose daughter frames in an inheritance structure; nominate lexical units evoking a newly created frame; and nominate examples and analyses.

AI chatbots based on LLMs obviously have limits. We consider only their possibilities as assistants, nominators, eliciting interlocutors for the fully engaged directorial linguist. The chatbot is no substitute for the trained construction grammarian or frame semanticist. Our initial forays into using chatbots showed instantly that they can be mistaken, for example, in proposing (a) *attribute frames* but with no core frame element to indicate an attribute associated with the entity; (b) *entity frames* whose list of lexical units is structured not by consistent lexicographic properties but rather by an ontology that derives from a simplistic checklist theory of meaning as composed of combinations of criterial properties; (c) *event frames* where core frame elements are missing, while other frame elements are inappropriately included in the frame even though they belong to a semantic frame on their own. This, again, highlights the need for careful human evaluation of the output provided by conversational AI.

We begin with a brief overview of the theory of Frame Semantics and its implementation in a computational lexicography project, "FrameNet." FrameNet is a database of words and phrases and their associated cognitive frames (Fillmore et al., 2003). Originally proposed for English, the FrameNet model has been expanded to other languages, including Spanish (Subirats & Petruck, 2003), Japanese (Ohara et al., 2004), Swedish (Dannéls et al., 2021), Brazilian Portuguese (Torrent et al, 2022a), German (Boas and Ziem, 2018), Chinese (You and Liu, 2005), Latvian (Gruzitis et al, 2018), and Korean (Hahm et al, 2020).

Frames can represent different types of cognitive structures, including events, entities, and the attributes associated with them. `Travel`[8] (Figure 1) is

---

[8] Following FrameNet convention, we indicate frame names in `Courier` font.

a prototypical eventive frame already defined in FrameNet. Each frame includes a definition describing the scene it represents, followed by participants and props related to the scene. These are called frame elements (FEs) and can be either core or noncore. Core FEs are those without which the frame cannot be instantiated. In the case of the `Travel` frame, core FEs include the **Traveler**, the **Destination**, and the **Mode_of_transportation**. Note that the fact that a FE is *core* does not mean that it will always be explicitly mentioned in discourse when the frame is somehow brought into play. Core FEs can be null-instantiated in the expressive performance, meaning that they can be inferrable. Noncore FEs, in turn, add circumstantial information to the frame and usually vary according to the type of frame. For example, eventive frames tend to have noncore FEs for Place and Time, while attributive frames have noncore FEs for Degree.

Frames also feature typed relations that connect them to other frames in the network – it is a FrameNET, after all. Relations include inheritance, subframe, using, precedes, perspective on, causative of, inchoative of, metaphor, and see also. The `Travel` frame instantiates three such relations. It inherits the

Figure 1 The `Travel` frame as defined for English.

Figure 1 (cont.)

Self_motion frame, indicating that the act of traveling is a more specific type of self-motion. It has one subframe, Setting_out, indicating that the act of traveling can be defined as being composed of at least one delimited subevent, namely that of starting the journey. Finally, it is typically connected to the `Tourism_scenario` frame, indicating that traveling usually refers to tourism.[9]

Because FrameNet was implemented as a lexicographic resource, frames usually have lexical units (LUs) associated with them. Those LUs are said to evoke the frame; that is, their presence in a text serves as a clue for the comprehender to evoke the whole conceptual structure represented in the frame. English verbs like *journey* and nouns like *expedition* do so for the `Travel` frame. According to FrameNet methodology (Fillmore et al., 2003; Ruppenhoffer et al., 2016), example sentences for each LU are extracted from corpora and annotated so as to attest to the analyses carried out when proposing each frame. In the Berkeley FrameNet database, there are seventy-one sentences annotated for *journey.n* evoking the `Travel` frame. Figure 2 shows a snippet of that annotated data.

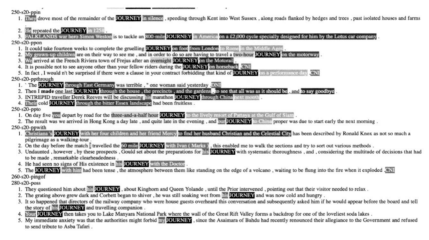

Figure 2 Snippet of the annotated data for the LU *journey.n* evoking the
`Travel` frame.

Note that, preceding each group of annotated sentences, there is a code indicating some syntactic patterns in which *journey.n* occurs. This information comes from the Word Sketch functionality of the Sketch Engine tool, as shown in Figure 3. This is to say that, when a lexicographer trained in developing FrameNet creates an LU in a frame, they will have conducted a previous corpus study to identify candidate patterns in which a given lemma evokes the frame in question. The kind of information provided by the Word Sketch tool is very helpful at this stage.

---

[9] For a description of the other frame-to-frame relations originally proposed for Berkeley FrameNet, see Ruppenhoffer and colleagues (2016). For a description of new types of relations proposed as a means to enrich FrameNet's database structure, see Torrent and colleagues (2022a).

Figure 3 shows that some of the word sketches provide cluster sentences that are more likely to instantiate the `Travel` frame than others: for example, the nouns modified by *journey.n* – the second column in the upper row of Figure 3 – seem to be all related to traveling. On the other hand, the pattern in which *journey.n* is accompanied by a possessor – the first column in the lower row – is not related to traveling: expressions such as *hero's journey*, *life's journey*, and *soul's journey* do not instantiate the `Travel` frame. Finally, some of the patterns seem to admit both: in the first column of the upper row, for example, *return.n* and *train.n* do adhere to the semantics of traveling, but *spiritual.a* does not.

The linguist building a frame uses both bottom-up and top-down approaches – see Torrent and colleagues (2014) for discussion. In terms of the bottom-up approach, the corpus study informs the definition of the frame and its FEs via the preliminary annotation of the example sentences found in the clusters provided; in terms of the top-down approach, lexicographers do have top-down knowledge about the domain for which the frame is being created, and accordingly refer to that knowledge when defining the scene and the participants in it.

The same kind of process applies to building eventive frames – such as `Travel` – and also to frames representing entities and attributes, such as the `Animals` and the `Color` frames (Figures 4 and 5). Yet the internal structure of entity and attribute frames tends to differ from the internal structure of eventive frames. Frames representing entities have, on average, 1.55 core FEs, while those representing attributes have 2.94 and those modeling events have 3.43. This may be regarded as a consequence of two factors. First, because event frames model cognitively relevant scenes in terms of their participants, it is reasonable that frames representing events have more FEs than frames representing entities. Second, because it is a lexicographic product, FrameNet is also influenced by both the syntactic behavior and the lexicalization patterns through which frames are expressed.

In summary, during the process of creating a frame, lexicographers must mobilize analytical capabilities that blend pattern recognition in data, common-sense knowledge, and knowledge about the existing network of frames, since newly created frames will be connected to existing frames. Moreover, AI LLM chatbots may be well designed to help in this process: The LLMs on which they are based, like all LLMs, create dense vector representations, also known as embeddings, for each lemma – or, in this context, word – based on the contexts in which those words appear in the training data. These word embeddings encode semantic and contextual information about the words. Accordingly, they

Figure 3 The Sketch Engine Word Sketch interface.

Figure 3 (cont.)

Animals

Figure 4 The `Animals` frame.

Color

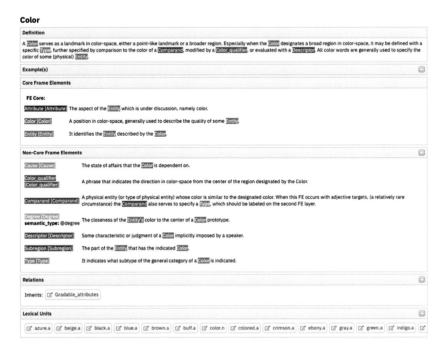

Figure 5 The `Color` frame.

may function as a more complex version of the Word Sketch tool. We demonstrate the utility of AI LLM chatbots through five experiments. In the first experiment, we probe their ability to augment existing frames in Berkeley FrameNet by suggesting additional LUs for them. In the second, since LLMs are trained on data in many languages, we show how they can be used to expand FrameNet into those languages. Our final three experiments assess their ability to propose new frames for the three most frequent types of frames in FrameNet: events, entities, and attributes.

Creating an entry for any FrameNet system is a big job. Although Berkeley FrameNet has created more than 1,200 frames for English, which can be evoked by more than 13,000 LUs, attested in more than 200,000 annotated sentences, yet very many cognitive frames – and the lexical units that evoke them – are absent from *all* present FrameNet systems.[10] To create a characterization of a frame, the researcher must first somehow hit upon a good candidate for inclusion in the relevant FrameNet and then review the relevant FrameNet systematically for associated frames, including frames from which the new frame might inherit structure, as well as other frames that might inherit structure from it. The researcher must analyze the structure and elements of the frame, their relationships, how that frame is evoked, lexical units that evoke it, and which phrases are associated with which elements of the frame. Typically, the researcher is also thinking about grammatical constructions that might evoke a frame. Naturally, the expansion of FrameNet has been slower than desired.

Since the early 2000s, initiatives and tools for expanding FrameNet have been developed by different means. Some FrameNets for other languages have been established in universities and research institutes around the world. Specific projects and initiatives have been proposed for aligning the resulting FrameNet databases. Software solutions have been developed for augmenting the resource coverage in both curated and data-driven approaches. The next section presents a review and some revisions of the computational tools devised for this purpose.

---

[10] Despite the fact that the FrameNets for other languages have been expanded from the original English one, some of them created frames for domains Berkeley FrameNet did not cover. Swedish FrameNet++, for example, has a large number of LUs for diseases, while FrameNet Brasil has created about 100 new frames and their respective LUs for modeling the domains of tourism and sports (Diniz da Costa et al., 2018).

5.1 Data-Driven Approaches to FrameNet Expansion

There are three dimensions, at least, along which FrameNet could be expanded.

1. *Creating new frames.* This is the most complex dimension. It entails conceptualizing not only the frame structure but also its frame elements and the initial set of lexical units evoking it. On top of that, proper care must be taken when wording a definition to avoid misinterpretations.
2. *New annotated examples* of known frames, known elements, and known LUs. This kind of expansion occurs when trained lexicographers engage in annotating full texts.
3. *Finding new LUs for existing frames.* This is the most common kind of expansion. It aims to increase the lexical coverage of the database. It typically explores large pools of external language resources in the hunt for new lexical units.

The reason why other language resources are especially useful for FrameNet expansion lies in the fact that FrameNet's coverage, in terms of domains and lexical units, is not that large, at least not for some data-driven applications. Different types of language resources call for different approaches to FrameNet expansion. For instance, dictionary-like resources can be used to obtain a list of new candidate LUs. Because LUs represent a single sense of a word or expression that evokes a frame X, when a dictionary is used to find a synonym, there is no guarantee that said synonym shares the same sense that evokes X. Thus, an appropriate way to refer to this synonym is "candidate LU." Resources that include sense information, such as WordNet, provide a better framework for constructing a list of candidate LUs, but still require some form of human assessment to guarantee that these candidates are actual LUs.

This procedure of finding candidate LUs in lexical resources has been extended to work with distributional resources, to expand LUs from one language to another, and, in the case of FrameNet+, to include a human-in-the-loop stage (Pennacchiotti et al., 2008; Hartmann & Gurevich, 2013; Pavlick et al., 2015). FrameNet+ is an augmented version of the Berkeley FrameNet 1.7 data release. It was built using a paraphrase database to generate possible correspondents to FrameNet's original *full-text* annotations, which were then evaluated according to their equivalence by crowdsourced workers. This comparison between original and paraphrase at the annotation level gives the workers a contextualized use of the lexical items, thus helping them assess whether the original and paraphrase evoke the same frame. If a paraphrase achieved both a high equivalency score and superior annotator agreement, it was used to obtain new LUs for the frames. In total, more than 22 K new Frame/ LU pairs were identified through this method, making it a good comparison dataset for one of the experiments in the present Element, discussed in Section 6.1.

An alternative approach for LU augmentation can be based on the "semantic frame induction task." The procedure of finding candidate LUs using external lexical resources exploits the relations between LUs evoking a frame and lexical items in other databases to find potential new LUs. Semantic frame induction, instead, treats all single or multiword expressions as LUs. The task consists of predicting the frame that a given LU evokes. The models designed for this task use vector representations of lexical items (usually from language models) and clustering techniques to make this prediction. These models are trained on the already-existing LUs from FrameNet databases.

One of the drawbacks of this type of model stems from the fact that FrameNet is treated as a static database. The prediction target in the semantic frame induction task is always an existing frame that cannot be changed. The assumption that, given a lemma, there must be a frame that it evokes in FrameNet is incorrect because researchers still work daily on the conceptualization of new frames. Moreover, on some occasions, frames are changed: for example, the frame might be changed to reflect more adequately the model of a domain. Because models for semantic frame induction are not designed to handle these cases, applying them in a FrameNet augmentation effort still demands careful evaluation of the results.

One model designed for the semantic frame induction task that attempts to mitigate the problems just discussed is the *Semi-supervised Deep Embedded Clustering with Anomaly Detection* (SDEC-AD) model. Instead of only predicting the frame evoked by an LU, it can also identify whether the frame evoked by that LU was modeled in FrameNet. The SDEC-AD model is a neural system that implements an autoencoder architecture and deep clustering techniques to implement a two-step frame induction workflow. The first step consists of identifying LUs that do not evoke any of the existing frames in FrameNet 1.7 (anomaly detection). After those are filtered out, the model predicts the frames evoked by the remaining LUs (Yong & Torrent, 2020). The central component in this induction workflow is the neural autoencoder, which provides enough information for anomaly detection and reduces the dimensions of the embeddings for the deep clustering used to identify the frame evoked by the LU.

The semi-supervised training of the autoencoder uses FrameNet+ data and is split into two phases, one to train the encoder and another to train the decoder. The embeddings for the LUs in FrameNet+ are obtained using the contextualized embeddings of their lemmas in example sentences and definitions generated by language models. These LUs (and their embeddings) can be partitioned into clusters, based on the frames that they evoked. This information is used to build a matrix of pairwise constraints, indicating which LUs should be part of the same cluster. In the first phase of the training pipeline, the encoder is trained to minimize an unsupervised divergence clustering loss and the semi-supervised constraint loss. This combined objective is computed using the matrix of pairwise constraints and the trainable weights representing the centroids of each frame in the embedding hyperspace. It jointly moves embeddings of the same frame closer to each other, while moving embeddings of different frames apart. This part of the training is the one that directly relates to predicting the frame evoked by an LU.

The second part of the SDEC-AD model trains the decoder to minimize the reconstruction loss – that is, the model needs to be able to reconstruct the embeddings transformed by the encoder back to the original forms in their LUs. The decoding performance over the training data is high in this phase, because only FrameNet+ LU embeddings are fed to the model. Intuitively, because the encoder brings embeddings from the same frame together, the loss should be smaller for those evoking a frame from FrameNet 1.7, even when they are not part of FrameNet+. The opposite is also valid: Embeddings from LUs that do not evoke one of the existing frames should be more distant and thus, more likely to be decoded with higher loss. Anomaly detection works by exploiting this bias. By setting a threshold for this loss, one can identify whether an LU evokes one of the existing frames or not.

Performance evaluation for the frame induction task uses common clustering metrics, namely the harmonic means of Purity and inverse Purity, and of BCubed precision and recall. These metrics were used to evaluate a variety of models trained for frame induction, using different techniques for clustering, ranging from hierarchical clustering (Anwar et al., 2019; Arefyev et al., 2019; Yamada et al., 2021) to the Chinese Whispers algorithm (Ribeiro et al., 2019) and, in the case of SDEC-AD, deep embedded clustering. The SDEC-AD model outperformed other models in all evaluation metrics for both LU clustering and identification of LUs that do not evoke an existing frame. It is important to note that models other than SDEC-AD are trained only to predict the frame evoked by an LU and, because of that, are not expected to perform as well as SDEC-AD in identifying LUs of frames that have not been modeled yet. These other approaches have their own contributions that can be generalized for the frame induction task as a whole. For instance, Yamada and colleagues (2021) show that when lemmas in an LU are masked to obtain their contextual embeddings, the weight given to word forms is decreased in favor of contextual information. For that reason, these embeddings are easier to partition between different word sense clusters, which are then clustered into frames. We move now to a brief discussion of models useful for different types of augmentation.

The tools discussed so far can be useful in an augmentation effort to find new LUs for existing frames. As previously mentioned, another form of augmentation consists in increasing the number of annotated examples in the database. The complexity of this task is significantly higher than the previous one, considering that FrameNet annotations have multiple layers. The models proposed for the SemEval-2019 Task 2 (QasemiZadeh et al., 2019) are useful for automatically labeling some, but not all, of the layers found in FrameNet's *full-text* annotation. The SemEval-2019 Task 2 is subdivided into three unsupervised tasks: (a) frame induction of verb lemmas; (b) frame semantic argument labeling, that is, frame element tagging; (c) case role labeling. Because frame semantic argument labeling entails frame induction, the SemEval-2019 models can be used to find new LUs for existing frames. In fact, SDEC-AD was compared to these models during its evaluation. The SemEval-2019 models have the advantage of being able to label FEs and generic semantic roles in text, with some restrictions. These outputs are a subset of a *full-text* annotation as found in FrameNets.

Frame semantic argument labeling or FE tagging in the SemEval-2019 models is treated as a clustering problem, making it possible to use techniques very similar to those used for predicting the frames evoked by LUs. For these tasks, it is convenient that the SemEval-2019 Task 2 is restricted to verbs. Accordingly, the models designed for this task only need to learn to induct frames for verb lemmas and, in the case of FE labeling, label prespecified verb-headed arguments. These argument structures were part of the training data, meaning that the systems did not have to actually identify the FEs in the entire input text. Instead, the semantic argument labeling task consists of identifying which FE corresponds to which argument of the verb. Since FEs are specified

per frame, the models need to work with a frame constraint while clustering
these elements.

All models submitted to SemEval-2019 Task 2 used the same approach
for FE tagging (Anwar et al., 2019; Arefyev et al., 2019; Ribeiro et al.,
2019). First, frame induction is executed over LUs. After that, verb
arguments are clustered for case role labeling. The rationale for clustering this way is that it is easier to partition the arguments into clusters of
generic semantic roles, such as *Agent* and *Theme*, simply because they
are not defined per frame like FEs. The final step assumes that FEs can
be inferred from the combined information of the frame evoked by the
verb and the generic semantic role of the arguments. This is done
by merging clusters from two tasks: frame induction and case role
labeling.

Evaluating FE tagging is like evaluating frame induction. The harmonic
means of Purity and inverse Purity, as well as BCubed precision and recall,
are used to measure the performance of different systems. Quality of
performance is an essential part of picking a model to augment
a FrameNet, but other factors also need to be considered. One of the big
limitations of the SemEval-2019 models derives from the fact that training
was restricted to verbs. In a real augmentation scenario, these models
would need to be paired with a corpus already annotated with argument
structures or another system that would automatically label those structures. Some limitations of the SemEval-2019 models are also found in
SDEC-AD. For example, all systems were trained only on the 1.7 release
of English FrameNet. Compared to some FrameNets, the 1.7 release has
a considerably higher number of frames and annotations. English is also
a high-resource language, which makes it more likely to find better contextualized embeddings for LUs. In spite of that, tools from the SemEval-
2019 represent a considerable improvement of the machine-based techniques for FrameNet augmentation, especially considering the complexity
of the tasks.

This brief discussion on data-driven approaches to FrameNet augmentation shows that techniques for finding new LUs have been explored more
extensively than techniques for creating new annotations. Labeling text to
create *full-text* annotations is a more complex task and manual work is still
required for a more grounded approach for this kind of expansion (Kim
et al., 2016).

The systems presented in this section present the researcher with two difficulties.
First, none of these systems addresses in full the task of complete frame creation,

that is, the task of defining a frame and its FEs and LUs. Second, researchers hoping to use any of these systems to add LUs to existing frames must struggle to learn and run the specialized software developed by each team. As we discuss in Section 6, AI LLM chatbots like OpenAssistant and ChatGPT can help the linguist finesse these two challenges. Before turning to the ways in which they can help the linguist finesse such challenges, we present one more tool for expanding FrameNet, namely "Lutma," which, unlike the other tools presented in this section, focuses precisely on helping users create *full* frame entries.

5.2 Lutma: A Frame Maker Tool

FrameNet Brasil has developed an app, "Lutma," to be used as a tool in expanding FrameNets and in building a Global FrameNet database. FrameNet Brasil describes Lutma as

> a collaborative, semi-constrained, tutorial-based tool for contributing frames and lexical units to the Global FrameNet initiative. The tool parameterizes the process of frame creation, avoiding consistency violations and promoting the integration of frames contributed by the community with existing frames. Lutma is structured in a wizard-like fashion so as to provide users with text and video tutorials relevant for each step in the frame creation process. (Torrent et al., 2022: 100)

Lutma guides the processes of both frame augmentation – that is, the insertion of new LUs into an existing frame – and frame creation. The parameters of its guidance were devised after an extensive study of the usual steps of frame augmentation and frame creation, and an extensive study of recurring patterns in the Berkeley FrameNet database. For example, Berkeley FrameNet has a pattern of typically occurring noncore FEs for each of its frame types – event, state, entity, attribute, and relation. Lutma is built upon and relies on such patterns.

As described in Torrent et al. (2022b), Lutma asks a user who wants to create a frame whether that frame can be evoked by some specific lexical material. If the user says yes and provides the LU, Lutma uses the lemma in that LU to check the existing Global FrameNet database to see whether the frame already exists in the database.[11] Lutma also checks external databases, such as Open Multilingual WordNet (Bond & Foster, 2013), for synonyms of the LU proposed by the user. If any coinciding lemma or near synonym is found, Lutma then shows the corresponding existing frames to the user, who must decide whether any of the existing frames

---

[11] https://globalframenet.org.

satisfies the need. If the user says no, the need is not satisfied, Lutma starts the process of guiding the user through each step of the frame creation process. The prototypical use flow asks the user to first choose the type of frame evoked by the LU: event, state, attribute, entity, or relation. The user can also select "other" if none of the standard types seems adequate. The user's choice causes Lutma to load a template that suggests noncore FEs and that then runs through some consistency checks, implemented as rules. Next, the user enters a frame name and a definition and moves forward to connect the new frame to one or more frames in the existing database. This exploration of connections is crucial: Once a frame-to-frame relation is created, Lutma can guide the user in creating core FEs as well, because those relations strongly suggest possible relations between the FEs. Figure 6 presents the Lutma workflow. Figure 7 presents an example of frame creation in Lutma.

Lutma makes the job of creating frames much more tractable and reliable, at least for researchers not extensively trained in FrameNet development, in part because of its wizard-like interface and tutorials. But it lacks a means of aiding the user in some crucial aspects, especially those involving pattern recognition. Hence, an AI system that could, for example, suggest new LUs, or aid in proposing new frames and FEs, may be quite useful.

Given that ChatGPT and OpenAssistant offer a conversational interface requiring no tech skills, could it take a place in the list of tools that help the linguist? In the next section of this Element, we present a series of five experiments aiming at probing the functionality of AI LLM chatbots in assisting the frame semanticist.

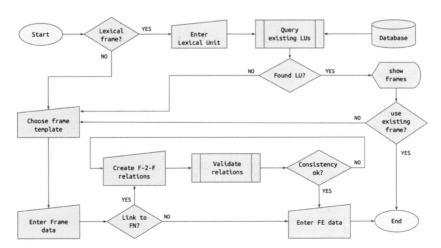

Figure 6 The frame creation process in Lutma (Torrent et al., 2022b).

Figure 7 Example case flow (Torrent et al., 2022b).

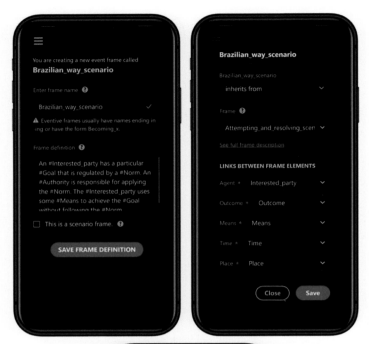

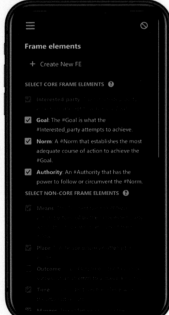

Figure 7 (cont.)

6 Prompt Engineering for Building FrameNet

At this point, one may ask why a frame semanticist would use an AI LLM chatbot instead of the other, established tools – such as Word Sketch, or SDEC-AD, or any of the systems in the SemEval 2019 Task 2. The answer is that ChatGPT and OpenAssistant produce very chatty, intuitive discourse. Because they work as chatbots, they require no coding knowledge from the linguist. It requires no coding skills to construct an elaborate setup and extensive querying of such AI chatbots. The linguist who wants to expand FrameNet can directly prompt the chatbot to work as a copilot, as an eliciting interlocutor, as an assistant in the task, and can instruct it in how to answer.

As discussed so far, building FrameNet involves a sequence of related tasks that results in a final product – the frame. The frame comprises:

- a frame name
- a frame definition
- a set of FEs, some of which are core
- a set of LUs evoking the frame
- corpus evidence supporting the analysis
- frame-to-frame relations connecting the newly created frame to the rest of the network

Notably, the frame name and definition are textual information. The FEs can be easily introduced by their names and definitions. But lexical units are better presented by their names and *part-of-speech*. In FrameNet, both FEs and LUs have other information – such as the definition of the LU, the type of FE, whether the LU incorporates an FE, and a group of sentences exemplifying the usage of the LU. Since there is a limit on the length of the prompt ChatGPT and OpenAssistant will accept, and this limit can impact performance, we have designed prompts that focus on only the most relevant information. We deflect noncore elements by filtering on the FE type, since FEs represent the core semantic space of a frame. The FEs incorporated by LUs are not consistently found in the database. When frames have a large number of lexical units, the prompt can be largely taken up by the mere presentation of the definition of the frame in the prompt, which presents operational problems. Lastly, the example sentences, in addition to potentially increasing the length of the input, represent corpus information that ChatGPT and OpenAssistant, as LLM-based chatbots, are expected to have, so we do not include them in the prompts.

In addition to this consideration of which parts of a frame to include in the prompt, there are two topics that require a fuller discussion: *full-text annotation* and *frame-to-frame relations*. Full-text annotations are corpus evidence derived from analyzing frames; they consist of texts and multiple layers of annotation, ranging from syntactic properties to frame elements. For linguists, this in-depth data is often indispensable to research on certain topics, such as valency patterns, but it is costly to create. Trying to pack full-text annotation into a relatively short prompt can produce dense and confusing language. Moreover, that information should already be implicitly present in LLMs' internal representations. Considering the vast amount of text on which LLMs are trained, we expect them to already represent, in one way or another, co-occurrence patterns of tokens, of types, and so on. Accordingly, the frame-builder is mercifully relieved of the task of providing this corpus evidence to AI LLM chatbots. Ideally, even brief prompts would serve to lead ChatGPT and OpenAssistant to help the linguist find new frames, LUs, and much more. Therefore, we have designed prompts so as to omit *full-text* annotations.

On the other hand, it can greatly help to include in the prompt one or more of the frame-to-frame relations that form the network. Frame-to-frame relations are graphical, and text has disadvantages in presenting graphical data, especially when there are many kinds of relations, many of them directional. Luckily, mere proximity of frames in the network can be used to provide adequate examples to AI LLM chatbots. For example, one can give the chatbot a frame X and ask it to create a corresponding perspective frame Y, and even prime the chatbot with a different, already-existing perspective frame. Similarly, one can prompt for frames related to X by inheritance, and prime the LLM with an existing child frame, asking it to produce a different child frame. Prompts in our experiments, reported in this section, exploit inheritance relations, but inheritance is only one illustrative possibility for prompt engineering. Other prompts could focus on other frame-to-frame relations.

In conclusion, to create prompt templates, we used frame and core FE names and definitions, LU names and their word classes, and some frame relations. We designed a Python script to bundle such information into multiple prompts for ChatGPT and OpenAssistant, thus partially automating some repetitive, regular labor in the task of creating frames. We discuss the resulting templates later in this section. Figure 8 presents a flowchart showing how the Python script adds pieces of frame data to the prompts. For each type of frame information, there is

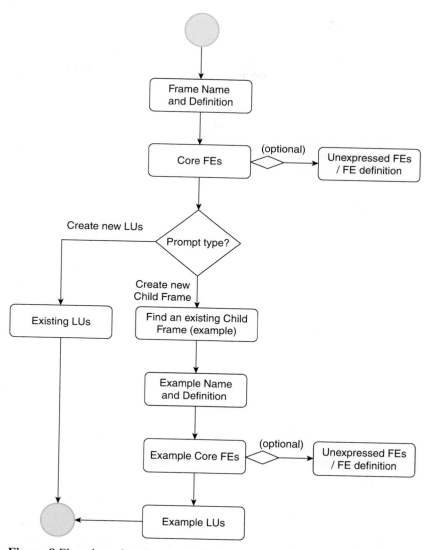

Figure 8 Flowchart showing the process of adding information to a prompt.

a single textual template that is filled during the process. Some of that frame information is included directly in the template, such as frame name and definition, and FE definitions. Other frame information needs more attention and tagging before being included it in the prompt; for example, core FE names and LUs are constrained by agreement and *part-of-speech* information, as will be discussed. The final part of the prompt contains a sentence requesting that the copilot either create a new frame or propose LUs. The chatbot is instructed by the template to provide its response in the form of a table or a JSON array. The sophisticated ability of the AI chatbot to present information in various formats greatly helps the further processing of the response it gives.

6.1 Experiment 1: FrameNet Augmentation via New Lexical Units

Our first experiment is designed to assess the chatbot's performance in proposing new lexical units, in English, for existing frames. The prompts provide, for each frame, a name, definition, a set of FEs, and a set of LUs. The LUs prime ChatGPT and OpenAssistant and prevent them from duplicating existing data. Consider our first prompt template in (37), where parameters are indicated with chevrons:

(37)   The semantic frame for "*<frame name>*" is defined as follows: "*<frame definition>*". Core frame elements in this frame are "*<core frame element names>*". *<Core frame element definitions>*. Words evoking this frame are the verbs *<verb lexical unit lists>*, adjectives *<adjective lexical unit lists>*, *<all other POS lexical units>*. Please propose 10 additional words that evoke the "*<frame name>*" semantic frame. Present them as a JSON array.

The prompt asks the chatbot to offer new LUs. If it asks for a low number of new LUs, the chatbots are likely to suggest the more frequent or obvious words, positively skewing their results but actually making them less helpful as a copilot. If it asks for a high number of new LUs, they will be much more exploratory, but at the cost of increased chance of error. In a preliminary assessment, we noted that requesting twenty-five candidate LUs, for some frames, caused a significant decrease in the quality of the response. This is expected, considering how varied frames can be. For example, the Animals frame is an entity frame that can potentially contain thousands of LUs. The Reassuring frame, on the contrary, models a scenario that, intuitively, is evoked by fewer lexical units. In Experiment 1, we asked ChatGPT and OpenAssistant to propose ten additional LUs, in order to prevent problems with certain frames while still allowing them some useful range in their proposals. For the sake of consistency, the requested number of examples is kept fixed at ten in our experiments, but in a real-life use case of the chatbot as a copilot, the user could vary this number.

Although the number of requested LUs is fixed in our experiments, other features of the prompt are controlled by the researcher. The researcher can vary the details of the frame description and the requested number of new LUs. For the existing frame, its number of core FEs and existing LUs can be taken from the dataset and used to help arrange frames into specific sets. The same can be done with their semantic families. These three factors – core FEs, existing LUs, and semantic families – can be isolated. We use them to measure the performance of the AI chatbots as copilots in different scenarios. More specifically, Experiment 1 is organized into twelve different scenarios, each corresponding to one combination of values on three different variables – *high* versus *low* FE count for the existing frame (HFE vs LFE), *high* versus *low* LU count for the existing frame (HLU vs LLU), and frame family (event, entity, attribute). For example, one scenario is (HFE, LLU, entity), while another is (LFE, LLU, attribute). The number of FEs or LUs for a frame is labeled "high" when that number is above the 75th percentile for all frames in FrameNet, and "low" when that number is below the 25th percentile. "High" versus "low" makes a difference because a model focused on the "high" end has more information to contextualize the frame structure, but still must suggest novel words, while a model focused on the "low" end has less information. The specificity of a frame has an effect on the number of frame elements: More elements suggest a more complex frame, containing more props. Finally, different families (event vs. entity vs. attribute) distinguish different semantic types of frames. A frame's position in a network depends on its family; for example, a frame's inheritance tree depends strongly on the family to which it belongs. By testing the performance of the chatbots contrastively in these twelve scenarios, we can answer three crucial questions:

1. How useful is each chatbot as a copilot for FrameNet augmentation via addition of lexical units?
2. How much does the amount of existing information influence the chatbot's effectiveness?
3. What type of information has greater influence over the quality of the responses?

The first step of the experiment was to sort frames into each of the twelve scenarios. Frames that were not part of one of the aforementioned families were excluded, along with those that were not part of the inferior and superior quartiles in number of LUs or FEs. We opted to randomly sample five frames from each scenario, resulting in a total of sixty distinct prompts generated using the experiment template. The number of examples per scenario was limited, based on the smallest of the twelve, which had only five frames. In all of its responses, as requested by the prompt, ChatGPT presented ten words that could be LUs, thus resulting in 600 items. Each candidate LU was first searched in FrameNet+ and then manually evaluated and judged as correct or incorrect by linguists trained in FrameNet building, including native speakers. Evaluating by scenario breaks the job down into much smaller clusters, which makes evaluation easier. It also allows the evaluation to be more precise, given that the performances of ChatGPT and OpenAssistant are likely to vary on the individual variables of frame family type, number of LUs, and number of FEs.

Table 1 presents the percentages of correct LUs proposed by ChatGPT, for each of the twelve scenarios. The numbers in parentheses are the percentages of the suggested words that are LUs in FrameNet+.

Some patterns are obvious from the responses. First, the *type* of frame has a significant influence on performance: Overall, LUs proposed by ChatGPT are more often judged correct by the linguist for entity and attribute frames than for event frames. This might be because event frames are generally more complex. Second, there is a trend having to do with low versus high LU count frames: For both LFE and HFE, the percentage of LUs proposed by ChatGPT that are then deemed correct by the linguists tends to be higher for HLU than for LLU. In contrast, for LLU, the percentage of LUs proposed by ChatGPT that are then deemed correct by the linguists is lower for HFE than for LFE. The number of frame elements does not seem to consistently influence the percentage of correct proposed words when frames have a lot of LUs. In fact, for event frames with a high number of LUs and FEs, all of the fifty suggested LUs were correct. On the opposite side of the spectrum, the lowest percentage of correct proposed LUs is also found for event frames, but in the HFE x LLU scenario. If we drill down to look specifically, at, for example, the Extradition and Commerce_collect frames, we find that for Extradition, ChatGPT suggests many words that would evoke neighboring frames in the same domain, such as *deportation.n* and *political asylum.n*,

Table 1 Percentage of correct English LUs proposed by ChatGPT. Percentages in parentheses indicate the percentage of proposed LUs that are already part of FrameNet+.

Frame Type	Scenario				Total
	LFE x LLU	LFE x HLU	HFE x LLU	HFE x HLU	
Event	.52 (.06)	.68 (.12)	.24 (.06)	1.00 (.01)	.61 (.08)
Entity	.60 (.00)	.92 (.10)	.66 (.04)	.88 (.04)	.76 (.04)
Attribute	.90 (.12)	.86 (.26)	.62 (.08)	.72 (.20)	.77 (.16)

or that are FEs, like *fugitive.n.* `Commerce_collect` is a perspective on `Commerce_money-transfer`, but the responses of the AI LLM chatbot include LUs from various frames in the commerce domain, without considering the different points of view. These facts can be seen as evidence that ChatGPT needs more LUs to handle structures that represent specific perspectives on a domain.

Table 2 presents the same percentages, but for LUs proposed by OpenAssistant. A first noticeable difference to the ChatGPT results is in the total percentage of individual families. There is a considerable gap in performance favoring ChatGPT. OpenAssistant's disadvantage is even larger for event frames. Other patterns found in Table 2 seem to indicate that despite their differences in performance, both chatbots are better copilots when more lexical information is contained in the prompt: The high LU count scenarios consistently outperform their low-count counterparts. The worst scenario for OpenAssistant is also the HFE x LLU one.

Interestingly, despite all of the observed correlations between the features of a frame and the number of correct LU suggestions a chatbot makes, ChatGPT's and OpenAssistant's suggestions overlap only somewhat with the lexical units already found in FrameNet+. For the scenario where the largest overlap with FrameNet+ is found, only 34 percent of OpenAssistant's LUs are shared. For ChatGPT, this number is 26 percent. Table 1 also shows cases of no overlap at all. This does not mean that ChatGPT is incorrect, as the other percentages disprove, nor that FrameNet+ has low coverage; rather, it simply shows that different approaches come up with different sets of possible LUs.

All of the results obtained in this experiment point to the conclusion that chatbots can serve as good copilots for linguists seeking to increase FrameNet LU coverage in English for already-existing frames.

Table 2 Percentage of correct English LUs proposed by OpenAssistant. Percentages in parentheses indicate the percentage of proposed LUs that are already part of FrameNet+.

Frame Type	Scenario				Total
	LFE x LLU	LFE x HLU	HFE x LLU	HFE x HLU	
Event	.28 (.08)	.42 (.02)	.22 (.02)	.50 (.22)	.35 (.08)
Entity	.44 (.00)	.86 (.10)	.32 (.04)	.88 (.06)	.62 (.05)
Attribute	.62 (.06)	.68 (.34)	.44 (.10)	.70 (.12)	.61 (.15)

1. In five of the twelve scenarios assessed for ChatGPT, more than 85 percent of the proposed lexical units were correct, and in only one scenario were fewer than 50 percent of the proposals correct.
2. Even in that one scenario, a real user interacting with the model can lower the number of requested LUs, thereby easily reducing the percentage of incorrect proposals.

OpenAssistant's performance is worse than ChatGPT's, but shows that even a smaller model can be useful for the linguist in some instances. It is also possible that with more prompt engineering and user interaction, OpenAssistant would provide better suggestions. In fact, this is a general condition that applies to all of our experiments and assessments. The chatbot is *never* an oracle speaking truth: Rather, it is an assistant *nominating* items to be considered by the specialist. The specialist user can respond critically very fast and thereby prevent incorrect proposals from entering FrameNet's database. The AI is good for some things, the human being for others. The future of this teamwork is the subject of this Element.

6.2 Experiment 2: FrameNet Expansion into Other Languages

Our second question was: Can AI LLM chatbots assist FrameNet's expansion to other languages? Researchers into Frame Semantics in other languages have routinely assumed that many if not most frames in the English FrameNet apply to those languages. Accordingly, the researcher might seek lexical materials in other languages that would evoke those same frames. One might begin simply by translating LUs from English into other languages, and asking whether those words in other languages evoke the same, or nearly the same, frame.

Compared to this method of extending FrameNet into other languages through brute-force lexical translation, AI LLM chatbots have the solid advantages of being more user-friendly and, as shown in Experiment 1, of being able to suggest sensible lexical units. Our second experiment is based on these advantages: it attempts to assess the ability of chatbots to propose lexical units in a different language for a frame that is already fully described in English.

The results of this second experiment might depend heavily on the non-English language chosen. We chose Brazilian Portuguese because the FrameNet Brasil database is rich, so we can compare the performances of the chatbots, the information in FrameNet+, and the information in FrameNet Brasil. This type of comparison adds another dimension to our investigation: we can check the performances of the chatbots against both FrameNet+ and FrameNet Brasil.

In Experiment 2, we used the same prompt as in Experiment 1, but then asked ChatGPT and OpenAssistant to produce LUs in Brazilian Portuguese:

(38)   Now list 10 unique words in Brazilian Portuguese that evoke this frame.

Experiments 1 and 2 are identical in the way they represent frame definitions, FEs, and existing LUs, so they can be directly compared to an extent. One distinction between these experiments is related to the prompts used. The prompt template (37) requests that the chatbot propose *additional* LUs in English; that is, the copilot should not list LUs already present in the frame description. On the other hand, the prompt requesting LUs in Brazilian Portuguese (38) does not restrict the LU list; as a result, in many instances, the ten Brazilian Portuguese "unique words" provided by the chatbot are actually translations of the English ones found in the frame description prompt. This is not a problem for Experiment 2 because many FrameNets were initially built by translating parts of the English database into other languages.

Table 3 shows the percentage of correct LU suggestions made by OpenAssistant in Brazilian Portuguese. These percentages are also organized in terms of the frame type and different combinations of FE and LU count, but instead of showing the percentages of LUs found in FrameNet+ in parentheses, it shows the percentages of LUs that exist in FrameNet Brasil (FN-Br).

In this experiment, the current limitations of OpenAssistant are clearly outlined: Only 42 percent of the LUs proposed for entity frames were correct. In the worst scenarios, only one in five of the candidate LUs were actual lexical units. This considerable drop in performance in comparison to Experiment 1 is explained by OpenAssistant's instruction training data. Of all of the messages used for training, only 3 K were in Brazilian Portuguese, compared to almost 72 K in English. Despite that, some of the patterns observed previously can still

Table 3 Percentage of correct Brazilian Portuguese LUs proposed by OpenAssistant. Percentages in parentheses refer to the proposed LUs that are part of FrameNet Brasil (FN-Br).

Frame Type	Scenarios				Total
	LFE x LLU	LFE x HLU	HFE x LLU	HFE x HLU	
Event	.30 (.02)	.24 (.08)	.20 (.00)	.28 (.04)	.25 (.03)
Entity	.24 (.02)	.56 (.10)	.20 (.06)	.70 (.12)	.42 (.07)
Attribute	.36 (.00)	.34 (.14)	.20 (.00)	.52 (.14)	.35 (.07)

Table 4 Percentage of correct Brazilian Portuguese LUs proposed by ChatGPT. Percentages in parentheses refer to the proposed LUs that are part of FN-Br.

Frame Type	Scenarios				Total
	LFE x LLU	LFE x HLU	HFE x LLU	HFE x HLU	
Event	.60 (.06)	.88 (.20)	.38 (.00)	.78 (.06)	.66 (.08)
Entity	.66 (.04)	.96 (.42)	.40 (.10)	.96 (.38)	.74 (.23)
Attribute	.86 (.02)	.98 (.60)	.42 (.02)	.84 (.24)	.77 (.22)

be seen in Table 3. For example, relatively speaking, the best scenarios were those where more lexical units were presented in the prompt. Since OpenAssistant still needs improvement in Brazilian Portuguese for this experiment, we now discuss ChatGPT's performance.

The percentages of human-evaluated correct frames in ChatGPT's responses in Experiment 2 are presented in Table 2. These results align with the ones from Experiment 1 and reinforce the observations made earlier. Once again, event frames seem to be harder for the model to deal with, although it performs slightly better with Portuguese, most likely because the model can generate words freely, without considering LUs already present in the prompt. Another trend that is also found in Experiment 2 with ChatGPT is the correlation of higher percentages with scenarios where frames have more LUs. However, there are considerable differences in the results, especially in the HFE x LLU scenario, which shows the lowest correct percentages in both experiments, but with different distributions. While in Experiment 1, the event frame results were considerably lower, in Experiment 2 they are almost uniform for all frame families. The entity family correctness rate fell from 66 percent to 40 percent, and ChatGPT did not propose a single correct LU for the Relational_political_locales frame. Once again, ChatGPT's processes do not consider the perspectival nature of the frame, that is, that it is evoked by LUs such as *capital.n* and *federal district.n*, which would adhere to the X of Y pattern (e.g., "capital of Brazil"). ChatGPT's suggestions did not fit the X of Y pattern, despite being related to political locales. Also worth noting is the frame Being_active, for which ChatGPT proposed only nouns as LUs, despite its being an attribute frame. This type of mistake, however, could possibly be reduced in a real-life use case, since the user can engineer a prompt that filters on *parts-of-speech*, for example.

What percentage of ChatGPT's suggestions of LUs was already contained in the existing, manually created, FN-Br database? For the families of Entity and Attribute frames, that percentage was relatively high: namely 23 and

22 percent, respectively. This is an increase, respectively, of 19 and 6 percentage points over the percentages obtained in Experiment 1, with English lexical units. These increases are probably explained by the absence of a restriction in the prompt on generating Brazilian Portuguese LUs that are already in the database. In any case, we see from these increased percentages some agreement between ChatGPT and human linguists when asked to propose LUs from scratch. This agreement is considerably higher in the two scenarios where frames have high LU counts: In that case, 31.6 percent of ChatGPT's suggested LUs were already present in the FN-Br database. In the low LU count scenarios, that overlap drops to only 4 percent.

We conclude that the results of Experiment 2 corroborate the results of Experiment 1, with some intricate differences. It is the case that AI LLM chatbots can work as copilots for linguists interested in finding lexical units in other languages based on English frame definitions. Their potential as useful tools is, however, limited by the training data. Moreover, the process of finding LUs in other languages also yields better results when frames have more lexical units, especially when the number of frame elements is also high. Once again, some limitations can be circumvented by careful prompt engineering, such as requiring specific *parts-of-speech* for LU suggestions.

We find specific areas of shortcoming for ChatGPT. For example, in more restricted spaces of a domain or certain perspectives, ChatGPT fails to capture the actual semantic space of the frame. OpenAssistant was highly limited by the training data in Brazilian Portuguese. In fact, the target language makes a difference: First, not all languages are supported in the current version of the chatbot. Second, due to variations in the language distribution of training data, performance in this kind of application may vary substantially by target language. Although we made explicit that this was the main problem for OpenAssistant, ChatGPT is also prone to this type of failure.

Once again, we reinforce that the linguist must play a supervisory role not only in creating prompts but also in interpreting results, because the target language can, both in its language features and in its cultural backgrounds, be more or less similar to English. For all these reasons, the linguist must keep an eye on the copilot. But with care, these AI LLM chatbots can be employed as useful copilots for expanding FrameNet via LU nomination.

The next sections discuss in detail the use of chatbots to augment FrameNet by creating new frames. The analyses conducted in the next three experiments are of a more qualitative nature, and explore the talkative nature of ChatGPT and OpenAssistant in a more extensive fashion.

6.3 Experiment 3: Entity Frame Building

For the experiments focusing on frame building, we guided ChatGPT and OpenAssistant with an initial prompt that is a variant of the prompt used in Experiment 1. The difference is that instead of asking the chatbot to provide a list of ten additional LUs evoking the frame in the prompt, we asked it to propose either (1) frames inheriting the original frame or (2) a related frame, given a new set of LUs.

Our first experiment of this kind asked ChatGPT and OpenAssistant to propose frames inheriting the Entity frame in FrameNet. The Entity frame is a very generic frame, under which 118 others are subsumed. The Entity frame is presented in Figure 9. Note especially the frames inheriting it. Although they do cover different groups of LUs that name different kinds of entities, nowhere in this network is there a place for nouns denoting deities, such as *goddess.n*, *deity.n*, and *saint.n*. Our prompt explored this lack of coverage in FrameNet. The resulting dialogue is reproduced in (39–40).

Figure 9 The Entity frame in FrameNet.

(39) USER: The semantic frame for "entity" is defined as follows: "This frame is for words that denote highly schematic entities". The semantic frame for "entity" has one core frame element: "entity". The definition of the "entity" frame element is as follows: "A thing (either abstract or physical) that exists with some degree of permanence". Words evoking this frame are the nouns "entity", "individual", "item", "object", "thing" and "what". Propose a semantic frame evoked by words such as "god", "saint", "deity" and "goddess".

(40) a. ChatGPT: A semantic frame evoked by words such as "god", "saint", "deity", and "goddess" could be called the "divine being" frame. The core frame element in this frame would be "divine being", with a definition similar to "a supernatural being or entity that is worshipped as having power over nature or human affairs". Words evoking this frame would include the nouns "god", "saint", "deity", "goddess", as well as other words that refer to supernatural beings that are worshipped or revered.

b. OpenAssistant: The semantic frames that may be evoked by these words include the following:
1. Entity Frame: These words refer to supernatural, powerful beings with various degrees of importance in different religious traditions. They can represent divine powers or deities.
2. Mythological Figure Frame: These words often relate to figures from mythology who have achieved saintly status due to their extraordinary feats, sacrifices, or devotion.
3. Worship Frame: These words can evoke a sense of reverence, veneration, and adoration towards the respective gods or saints, often associated with rituals and practices.
4. Symbolic Frame: Some people view these terms symbolically, associating them with higher ideals, moral values, or spiritual principles that transcend everyday life.

The answer provided by ChatGPT includes information that could be helpful in creating the frame, despite the fact that this assistant did not provide a definition for the Divine_being frame proposed. On the other hand, the core FE proposed would most likely be included in the frame if it had been created by a human lexicographer alone. Such an FE is incorporated in LUs evoking the Divine_being frame. A brief corpus study conducted using the WordSketch tool shows that nouns such as the ones in the prompt are frequently associated with modifiers indicating the religion with which the divine being is associated, as shown in Figure 10.

Accordingly, a linguist building the Divine_being frame might wonder whether to add another core FE to this frame, namely Religion. The linguist would need to consider other LUs and conduct a more comprehensive corpus study.

modifiers of "deity"		
patron	7	9.1 ···
tutelary	3	8.7 ···
primordial	3	8.2 ···
primeval ···		
omnipotent	2	8.0 ···
minoan	4	7.9 ···
benevolent	3	7.9 ···
falcon	2	7.6 ···
celtic	4	7.5 ···
ram	2	7.3 ···
hindu	2	7.0 ···
tribal ···		
pagan	2	6.8 ···
supreme	3	6.7 ···
twin	3	6.1 ···
greek	4	5.7 ···
ancient ···		
male	6	5.4 ···
female ··· powerful ··· central ···		
lesser	2	5.2 ···
animal	2	4.8 ···
minor	2	4.1 ···
single	6	3.7 ···
various ··· local ··· particular ···		
several ··· major ··· different ···		
other ··· own ··· old ···		
more ···		
water	2	2.8 ···

modifiers of "saint"		
patron	99	12.6 ···
the patron saint of		
plaster	9	9.0 ···
virgin	5	8.2 ···
jesuit	3	7.8 ···
bohemian	3	7.7 ···
celtic	5	7.6 ···
holy	4	6.8 ···
catholic	4	6.1 ···
favourite	5	5.6 ···
woman	3	4.6 ···
royal	3	4.6 ···
english	3	3.2 ···
local ··· great ··· other ···		

modifiers of "goddess"		
snake	5	8.6 ···
hindu	4	8.5 ···
minoan	6	8.4 ···
fertility	6	8.2 ···
screen	8	7.8 ···
mother	14	7.5 ···
the mother goddess		
god ···		
celtic	4	7.5 ···
greek	14	7.5 ···
greek goddess of		
egyptian ···		
sky	4	7.4 ···
sun ···		
earth	3	6.0 ···
green	5	6.0 ···
sex	4	5.3 ···
roman	4	5.1 ···
great	4	4.7 ···
female	3	4.5 ···
great ···		

Figure 10 WordSketches for the nouns *deity*, *saint*, and *goddess* in the British National Corpus.

OpenAssistant, in turn, provides an answer that lists four frames that could be somehow associated with a frame evoked by the LUs in the prompt. For each of them, it provides a definition whose wording sounds less FrameNet-like than the one provided by ChatGPT. This raises the question of whether OpenAssistant, which is based on an open source LLM, could be trained on FrameNet data so that it could enhance its functionality as a copilot. This question is under investigation as this Element is being written and we plan to report on it soon.

Continuing the experiment, we replied to both ChatGPT and OpenAssistant with the prompt in (41), which generated the answer in (42).

(41)   USER: Now, please propose semantic frames for other kinds of entities. Present them as a table in which columns are "Frame Name", "Frame Definition", "Frame Elements", "Frame Element Definition", "Words evoking the frame".

(42)   a. ChatGPT:

Frame Name	Frame Definition	Frame Elements	Frame Element Definition	Words Evoking the Frame
Physical entity	This frame is for words that denote concrete, physical objects or things	Physical entity	A concrete, physical object or thing that exists in space and time	"rock", "tree", "table", "car", "building"
Abstract entity	This frame is for words that denote abstract concepts or ideas	Abstract entity	An abstract concept or idea that exists without a physical form	"truth", "love", "justice", "beauty", "happiness
Social entity	This frame is for words that denote groups of individuals who interact with each other	Social entity	A group of individuals who interact with each other and have some common characteristics or goals	"family", "team", "company", "government", "society"
Natural entity	This frame is for words that denote natural phenomena or processes	Natural entity	A phenomenon or process that occurs in nature and is not the result of human activity	"storm", "earthquake", "evolution", "photosynthesis", "ecosystem

b. OpenAssistant: Certainly, here's an example of a table displaying the requested information on different types of entities and their corresponding frames:

Frame Name	Frame Definition	Frame Elements	Frame Element Definition	Words Evoking the Frame
Object	A tangible entity that occupies space and can be perceived through sensory modalities	Item, thing, possession, matter	Physical object, material possessions	chair, car, desk, TV, phone
Concept	An abstraction representing a set of related ideas or notions	Idea, principle, conceptualization	Abstract idea, mental construct	justice, democracy, love, truth, beauty, freedom
Event	Something that happens within a specific timeframe and involves interactions between entities	Occurrence, occurrence event, happening	Temporal sequence of events	accident, performance, wedding ceremony, meeting, birth
Group/Organization	A collective body comprising individuals united by common goals, interests, or purposes	Institution, association, club	Social grouping, human organization	company, family, school, government, union
Process/Procedure	A series of steps or actions taken to achieve a particular outcome or result	Algorithm, method, technique, protocol	Sequential task-oriented process	recipe, formula, operation, algorithm, project management plan
Emotion	A subjective experience characterized by distinct physiological and psychological states	Feeling, affect	Internal emotional state	happiness, sadness, anger, surprise, fear, disgust, contempt

Note that, at first glance, the groupings seem to make sense. Nonetheless, this sense-making is not grounded on FrameNet principles and methodology for either chatbot. Rather, the groupings make sense because they are similar to a top ontology for entities. FrameNet is a lexicographic resource, meaning that the reasons supporting the decision-making process on the frame membership of a lexical unit must take into consideration how the LU surfaces in corpora. That said, while nouns like *love* and *happiness* presuppose a scene involving an **Experiencer** and the **Stimulus** producing the emotion they lexicalize, others like *beauty* require an **Entity** which will be assigned such a feature. An even clearer example of the bad performance of ChatGPT is the list of LUs it suggests in (42a) for evoking a frame for natural entities: with the exception of *ecosystem*, all of the words refer to events and processes, not entities at all.

OpenAssistant's performance in (42b) also has problems. While it makes the same mistake of mixing nouns denoting emotions with others indicating attributes, it includes a frame for `Event` and one for `Process/Procedure` in the list.

One possible reason for ChatGPT's and OpenAssistant failure may be the very generic nature of the `Entity` frame used in the prompt. Both the frame definition and the LUs evoking the frame are very generic. In other words, we hypothesize that, whatever might be the nature of the representations the LLM builds for the words it processes, representations for words like *thing* and *entity* may not be highly informative for the task. To test this hypothesis, we prompted the LLM-based chatbots once again – at a different moment in the chats, that is, not right after the answer in (42) – with a prompt based on a frame inheriting `Entity`, namely the `Artifact` frame. (43) is the new prompt, (44a) is ChatGPT's reply to it, and (44b) is OpenAssistant's.

(43)   The semantic frame for "artifact" is defined as follows: "An Artifact is deliberately made or modified by an intelligent entity to be put to a certain kind of Use. Various properties of the Artifact may be specified, such as its Creator, Time_of_creation, Name, Type, and the Material of which it is composed. The Artifact may or may not be a physical entity." The semantic frame for "artifact" has one core frame element: "artifact". The definition of the "artifact" frame element is as follows: "This FE identifies the entity or substance that is designed to have a particular Use. This can refer to physical artifacts, like a mug or computer monitor, or a digital artifact, such as a website or document.". Words evoking this frame are the nouns "artifact", "biotechnology", "technology". The frame for "information display" inherits the frame for "artifact" and is defined as "A man-made artifact, digital or physical, which is used to display information presented via the object.". The "information display" frame has one core frame element, "display", which is defined as "This FE identifies the entity or substance that is designed to have a particular Use". The "information display" frame is evoked by words such as the nouns "board" and "monitor". Please propose semantic frames for other kinds of artifacts. Present them as a table in which columns are "Frame Name", "Frame Definition", "Frame Elements", "Frame Element Definition", "Words evoking the frame".

(44)   a. ChatGPT: Here are some proposed semantic frames for different kinds of artifacts:

Frame Name	Frame Definition	Frame Elements	Frame Element Definition	Words Evoking the Frame
Musical Instrument	A man-made artifact designed for creating music.	Instrument	This FE identifies the entity or substance that is designed to create music.	Guitar, Piano, Drums
Tool	A man-made artifact designed to assist in completing a task.	Tool	This FE identifies the entity or substance that is designed to assist in completing a task.	Hammer, Screwdriver, Wrench
Weapon	A man-made artifact designed to harm or kill living beings.	Weapon	This FE identifies the entity or substance that is designed to harm or kill living beings.	Gun, Knife, Bow and Arrow
Transportation	A man-made artifact designed to transport people or goods from one place to another.	Vehicle, Cargo	Vehicle: This FE identifies the entity or substance that is designed to transport people. Cargo: This FE identifies the entity or substance that is designed to transport goods.	Car, Train, Ship
Clothing	A man-made artifact designed to cover the body or protect it from the environment.	Garment	This FE identifies the entity or substance that is designed to cover or protect the body.	Shirt, Pants, Coat
Housing	A man-made artifact designed for living or working in.	Room, Building	Room: This FE identifies the entity or substance that is designed for living or working in. Building: This FE identifies the entity or substance that is made up of multiple rooms designed for living or working in.	House, Apartment, Office Building

Note: The words evoking each frame are not exhaustive and can be expanded based on the context and usage.

b. OpenAssistant: Here are some example tables illustrating different types of artifacts, including their frame names, definitions, elements, and evoking words:

Table 1: Physical artifacts

Frame Name	Frame Definition	Frame Elements	Frame Element Definition	Words Evoking the Frame
Tool	A device specifically designed to aid in performing a task	Handle, blade, motor	Properties that enable efficient performance of a specific task	Knife, screwdriver, drill
Vehicle	A machine designed for transporting persons or goods over land, water, air, or space	Wheels, wings, engines	Characteristics enabling movement and load capacity	Car, plane, train
Container	A receptacle with a lid or cover used for storing, carrying, or displaying items	Lid, handle, body	Qualities facilitating protection, accessibility, and organization of contents	Box, bag, bottle

Table 2: Digital artifacts

Frame Name	Frame Definition	Frame Elements	Frame Element Definition	Words Evoking the Frame
Software	Computer instructions stored on a medium and executed by a processor to perform tasks or operations	Code, algorithms, libraries	Functional components contributing to desired application behavior	Operating system, program, app
Website	Collection of interlinked hypertext documents accessed via the Internet through a browser	Pages, links, multimedia content	Attributes supporting presentation, navigation, and interaction	Webpage, menu, button
Data set	Organized collection of facts, figures, or statistics represented in a structured format suitable for analysis or processing	Columns, rows, fields	Components allowing storage, retrieval, manipulation, and output of data values	Database record, spreadsheet row, chart series

Note: Each table presents only a few representative examples; many more variations and subtypes exist within each category depending on contextual usage.

Looking at (44a) first, we can see that, this time, the frames proposed by ChatGPT are rather closer to the ones a linguist would propose for FrameNet. Actually, two of them – the one for weapon and the one for clothing – are almost a perfect match to frames already existing in FrameNet. As for OpenAssistant's performance in (44b), although the prose of the FE definition does not conform to what is expected, the performance also improves. It is also impressive that this chatbot even suggests a split between physical and digital artifacts. Those improved results reinforce the importance of prompt engineering for AI LLM chatbots to provide more useful answers to the linguist. Interestingly, the fact that prompt engineering has such an influence on the output of the chatbot used as a tool for linguistic analysis reinforces the fact that those models do not have proper understanding of the language. In other words, the fact that an AI LLM chatbot may be useful as a tool for linguistic analysis does not mean it has language understanding capabilities.

In the next experiment, we use the same process to prompt for attribute frames.

6.4 Experiment 4: Attribute Frame Building

The second largest cluster of frames in FrameNet consists of frames indicating characteristics and features of entities: There are 202 frames related to the `Attributes` frame in the Berkeley FrameNet 1.7 data release. The `Attributes` frame is nonlexical, meaning that it has no LUs associated with it. Therefore, we chose instead the `Gradable_attributes` frame as the basis of our prompt because, although it is also nonlexical, it is the immediate mother of several lexical frames. See Figure 11 for the `Gradable_attributes` frame. We prompted ChatGPT and OpenAssistant right after (42).

Note that, due to the lack of LUs evoking the mother frame in the inheritance relation, the prompt presented in (45) is slightly different from the standard used so far. It provided both chatbots with the mother frame name, definition, and list of core FEs. For the daughter frame, we provided the frame name and definition, as well as the core FEs and LUs evoking it. ChatGPT's answer is shown in (46a) and OpenAssistant's in (46b).

(45)   USER: Similarly, there is also a frame for "gradable attributes", whose defin-
         ition is as follows: "An Entity has an implicit Value for an Attribute. Degree
         expresses either explicit comparison or the deviation of the Value when
         compared with other entities of similar kind. The Value may hold only relative

Gradable_attributes

Definition

An Entity has an implicit Value for an Attribute. The Degree expresses either explicit comparison or the deviation of the Value when compared with other entities of similar kind. The Value may hold only relative to a particular Time or in particular Circumstances.

Example(s)

Core Frame Elements

FE Core:

Degree [Degree]
excludes: Value
semantic_type: @degree

A modifier expressing the deviation of the Value from the norm or from the value for another Entity.

Entity [Entity]

The Entity for which a particular gradable Attribute is appropriate and under consideration.

FE Core-Unexpressed:

Attribute [Attribute]

The feature of an Entity which is under discussion.

Value [Value]

The generally implicit Value of the Attribute.

Non-Core Frame Elements

Circumstances
[Circumstances]

Some specification of the circumstances under which the Entity has a particular Value for the Attribute.

Place [Place]

The location where the Entity is has the Attribute to a given Degree.

Time [Time]
semantic_type: @time

The Time during which the Entity is in the state of having a particular Value for the Attribute.

Relations

Inherited By:	Abundance · Addiction · Artificiality · Being_active · Being_at_risk · Being_dry · Being_rotted · Being_wet · Biological_urge · Body_description_holistic · Body_description_part · Capability · Certainty · Chemical-sense_description · Chemical_potency · Color · Color_qualities · Compatibility · Completeness · Correctness · Desirability · Difficulty · Familiarity · Frequency · Fullness · Gradable_artistic_quality · Inclination · Intoxication · Judgment_of_intensity · Level_of_light · Likelihood · Lively_place · Luck · Margin_of_resolution · Measurable_attributes · Medical_conditions · Notability · Obscurity · Obviousness · Personal_success · Position_on_a_scale · Prominence · Risky_situation · Sharpness · Similarity · Social_behavior_evaluation · Suitability · System_complexity · Taking_time · Usefulness · Wealthiness
Inherits:	Attributes
Used By:	Extreme_point · First_rank

Figure 11 The `Gradable_attributes` frame in FrameNet.

to a particular Time or in particular Circumstances.". Core frame elements in this frame are "Entity" and "Degree". Core unexpressed frame elements are "Attribute" and "Value". The "color" frame inherits the "gradable attributes" frame. Core frame elements in the "color" frame are "Entity" and "Color". The "color" frame is evoked by adjectives such as "azure", "beige", "blue", "orange", "pink", "red", among others. Now, propose other semantic frames inheriting the "gradable attributes" frame. Present them as a table in which columns are "Frame Name", "Frame Definition", "Frame Elements", "Frame Element Definition", "Words evoking the frame".

(46)   a. ChatGPT:

Frame Name	Frame Definition	Frame Elements	Frame Element Definition	Words Evoking the Frame
Size	This frame is for words that describe the dimensions or magnitude of an object or concept	Entity	A thing (either abstract or physical) that exists with some degree of permanence	"big", "small", "tiny", "gigantic", "huge"
Age	This frame is for words that describe the length of time an entity has existed or been in use	Entity	A thing (either abstract or physical) that exists with some degree of permanence	"old", "new", "young", "ancient", "mature"
Temperature	This frame is for words that describe the degree of hotness or coldness of an entity	Entity	A thing (either abstract or physical) that exists with some degree of permanence	"hot", "cold", "warm", "frigid", "boiling"
Brightness	This frame is for words that describe the intensity of light emitted or reflected by an entity	Entity	A thing (either abstract or physical) that exists with some degree of permanence	"bright", "dim", "glowing", "pale", "radiant"
Loudness	This frame is for words that describe the intensity of sound produced by an entity	Entity	A thing (either abstract or physical) that exists with some degree of permanence	"loud", "quiet", "soft", "deafening", "hushed"

b. OpenAssistant: Yes, certainly! Here are some examples of semantic frames inherited from the "Graduated Attributes" frame along with their core elements and trigger words:

Frame Name	Frame Definition	Frame Elements	Frame Element Definition	Trigger Word(s)
Size	Refers to the physical dimensions of an object, typically its length, width, and height.	Length, breadth, depth	Measurements of size	tall, short, big, small
Volume	Represents the amount of space occupied by an object, often expressed in cubic units (e.g., cm^3).	Cubic measure, capacity, volume	Amount of space occupied by an object	large, spacious, roomy
Intensity	Denotes the strength or power of something, measured on a scale such as a magnitude scale or intensity scale.	Magnitude, degree, level	Strength or power of something	strong, weak, powerful, mild
Weight	Reflects the gravitational force acting upon an object, usually measured in units of mass (e.g., kg).	Gravitational force, mass	Amount of matter present in an object	light, heavy, dense
Speed	Describes how fast an object moves over a given distance.	Distance traveled per unit time	Movement rate, velocity	Quick

From the beginning, once again, the ontology-like aspect of the answer surfaces clearly: All of the frames proposed by both chatbots are types of attributes that entities can show. The frame definitions follow the same logic. For ChatGPT, however, all proposed frames have only one FE, the **Entity**, whose definition is copied from that of the Entity frame, which ChatGPT had seen in a previous prompt in this sequence – (39). Instead of changing the prompt and starting a new instance of the interface, this time we decided to emulate a continuation of the dialogue with the assistant, so as to assess to what extent its propagated ability to correct itself would apply. The continuation of the conversation is presented next:

(47)   USER: Why did you propose only one frame element per frame?

(48)   ChatGPT: I proposed only one frame element per frame because each of the frames I listed describes a specific attribute or property of an entity, and in each case the entity is the focus of the frame. In other words, the entity is the thing that has the attribute or property described by the frame, and the attribute or property itself is the core frame element. For example, in the "size" frame, the entity is the thing that has a certain size, and the size itself is the core frame element. Similarly, in the "age" frame, the entity is the thing that has a certain age, and the age itself is the core frame element. I chose to focus on only one frame element per frame in order to clearly illustrate the relationship between the entity and the attribute or property being described.

(49)   USER: But, for the "color" frame, there were two core frame elements: "entity" and "color". Shouldn't the frames you propose also have another frame element?

(50)   ChatGPT: You are correct that the "color" frame has two core frame elements: "entity" and "color". This is because the "color" frame is inherited from the "gradable attributes" frame, which has two core frame elements: "entity" and "degree". The "color" frame maintains these two core frame elements and adds an additional one, "color", to specify the specific attribute being described. In the frames that I proposed, it is not necessary to include additional frame elements because each frame describes a specific attribute or property of an entity, and the attribute or property itself serves as the core frame element. For example, in the "size" frame, the attribute being described is size, so there is no need for an additional frame element to specify the attribute. Similarly, in the "age" frame, the attribute being described is age, so there is no need for an additional frame element to specify the attribute. However, if desired, additional frame elements could be added to these frames to provide more detailed information about the attribute being described. For example, the "size" frame could include an additional frame element called "unit of measure" to specify the units in which size is being measured (e.g. inches, feet, centimeters, etc.).

(51)   USER: But doesn't "color" also describe an attribute of the "entity"? And don't the frames you proposed also inherit "gradable attributes"? So, why do they only have one core frame element, while color has two?

(52)   ChatGPT: Yes, "color" does describe an attribute of the entity. The "color" frame inherits the "gradable attributes" frame, which has two core frame elements: "entity" and "degree". The "color" frame maintains these two

core frame elements and adds an additional one, "color", to specify the specific attribute being described. In contrast, the frames I proposed do not inherit the "gradable attributes" frame and therefore do not have the same core frame elements. Instead, each of the frames I proposed describes a specific attribute or property of an entity, and the attribute or property itself serves as the core frame element. For example, in the "size" frame, the attribute being described is size, so the "size" frame has only one core frame element, "size". Similarly, in the "age" frame, the attribute being described is age, so the "age" frame has only one core frame element, "age". In summary, the "color" frame has two core frame elements because it inherits the "gradable attributes" frame and adds an additional frame element to specify the specific attribute being described. In contrast, the frames I proposed do not inherit the "gradable attributes" frame and therefore have only one core frame element, which is the attribute or property being described.

Note that, in (48), ChatGPT's response does not answer the question; moreover, it contradicts itself. First, it says that **Entity** was the only core FE proposed because it is the focus of the frame. In the following sentence, however, it states that the attribute or property itself is the core FE. The remainder of (48) only increases the confusion, revealing that, although the tool may be useful for augmenting existing frames with new LUs – as results from Experiment 1 and 2 suggest – the kinds of representations on which its performance was based for that task are not useful for the problem presented in (47). It is possible that, because the prompt in (45) – which started the request for frames inheriting `Gradable_attributes` – was presented to ChatGPT in the same chat instance where prompt (41) was inserted – asking for frames inheriting the `Entity` frame, the assistant persisted in the mistake, since the "memory" of the **Entity** FE was very strong in the chat history. To test this question, we started a *new instance* of ChatGPT and inserted, as the first prompt in the conversation, the one in (53), which generated the answer in (54a). We did the same for OpenAssistant, whose answer is shown in (54b).

(53) USER: There is a semantic frame for "gradable attributes", whose definition is as follows: "An Entity has an implicit Value for an Attribute. Degree expresses either explicit comparison or the deviation of the Value when compared with other entities of similar kind. The Value may hold only relative to a particular Time or in particular Circumstances.". Core frame elements in this frame are "Entity" and "Degree". Core unexpressed frame elements are "Attribute" and "Value". The "color" frame inherits the "gradable attributes" frame. Core frame elements in the "color" frame are "Entity" and "Color". The "color" frame is evoked by adjectives such as "azure", "beige", "blue", "orange", "pink", "red", among others. Now, propose other semantic frames inheriting the "gradable attributes" frame. Present them as a table in which columns are "Frame Name", "Frame Definition", "Frame Elements", "Frame Element Definition", "Words evoking the frame".

(54)   a. ChatGPT:

Frame Name	Frame Definition	Frame Elements	Frame Element Definition	Words Evoking the Frame
Temperature	An Entity has an implicit Value for Temperature. Degree expresses either explicit comparison or the deviation of the Value.	Entity, Degree	Entity: The object or substance that has a temperature. Degree: The degree of hotness or coldness of the entity relative to other entities of similar kind.	Hot, cold, warm, cool, freezing, boiling, scorching, chilly, icy, torrid, arctic, frigid, lukewarm
Brightness	An Entity has an implicit Value for Brightness. Degree expresses either explicit comparison or the deviation of the Value.	Entity, Degree	Entity: The object or substance that has a brightness value. Degree: The degree of brightness of the entity relative to other entities of similar kind.	Bright, dim, radiant, luminous, dazzling, glowing, brilliant, shiny, glossy, dark, dull, opaque, translucent
Loudness	An Entity has an implicit Value for Loudness. Degree expresses either explicit comparison or the deviation of the Value.	Entity, Degree	Entity: The object or substance that has a loudness value. Degree: The degree of loudness of the entity relative to other entities of similar kind.	Loud, soft, noisy, silent, deafening, muted, hushed, quiet, muffled, piercing, booming, thunderous
Size	An Entity has an implicit Value for Size. Degree expresses either explicit comparison or the deviation of the Value.	Entity, Degree	Entity: The object or substance that has a size value. Degree: The degree of size of the entity relative to other entities of similar kind.	Big, small, tiny, large, colossal, immense, diminutive, compact, enormous, microscopic, gargantuan, puny
Intensity	An Entity has an implicit Value for Intensity. Degree expresses either explicit comparison or the deviation of the Value.	Entity, Degree	Entity: The object or substance that has an intensity value. Degree: The degree of intensity of the entity relative to other entities of similar kind.	Strong, weak, powerful, feeble, intense, subdued, forceful, gentle, potent, faint, vibrant, mild

Sweetness	An Entity has an implicit Value for Sweetness. Degree expresses either explicit comparison or the deviation of the Value.	Entity, Degree	Entity: The object or substance that has a sweetness value. Degree: The degree of sweetness of the entity relative to other entities of similar kind.	Sweet, sour, bitter, sugary, tangy, acrid, cloying, tart, pungent, zesty, sharp, saccharine
Texture	An Entity has an implicit Value for Texture. Degree expresses either explicit comparison or the deviation of the Value.	Entity, Degree	Entity: The object or substance that has a texture value. Degree: The degree of texture of the entity relative to other entities of similar kind.	Smooth, rough, soft, coarse, grainy, silky, velvety, bumpy, lumpy, fuzzy, prickly, wiry

b. OpenAssistant: Here's one possible answer:

Frame	Frame Definition	Frame Elements	Frame Element Definition	Words Evoking the Frame
Loudness	An entity (e.g., sound) can be judged as having different levels of loudness.	Amount of energy perceived by human ear over time	Auditory sensation resulting from a certain acoustic power that a person hears	Loud, quiet, soft, silence, volume
Height	An object or creature has a specific height.	Vertical distance between the lowest point and the highest point of an object/ creature	Distance measured along the vertical axis	Tall, short, low, high
Weight	An object or living being has a measurable mass.	Measured force exerted on another body due to gravity	Force measured under the influence of Earth's gravity	Heavy, light, weightless
Temperature	The measure of hotness or coldness for an environment or object.	Thermal sense experienced by objects or living organisms	Sensory perception related to heat flow	Hot, warm, cold, chilly

For this new prompt, the problems with OpenAssistant's performance remain the same: it provides good frame names and definitions, a good list of candidate LUs, but does not conform to the expected when it comes to listing FEs and defining them.

As for ChatGPT, as much as the test with the fresh chat instance generates a different answer, the problem remains to some extent. ChatGPT now relies exclusively on the `Gradable_attributes` frame for proposing the frames inheriting it and does not capture the consequences of the inheritance relation between this frame and the `Color` frame, also present in the prompt in (53). More specifically, the frames proposed in (54a) do not feature a FE inheriting the core unexpressed **Attribute** FE in the `Gradable_attributes` frame. Core unexpressed FEs are defined in FrameNet methodology as "FEs that behave like core frame elements in the frame where they are marked as Core-unexpressed but which, counter to expectation, may not be used for annotation in descendants of that frame. Frame elements marked as core-unexpressed will thus not necessarily be listed among the FEs in descendant frames" (Ruppenhofer et al., 2016: 25).

In other words, in FrameNet methodology, core unexpressed FEs are resources adopted in the model to express the fact that, when some highly abstract frames such as, for example, `Intentionally_act` are created, they must feature FEs such as **Act**, for lexicographic reasons. Because this frame is evoked by LUs such as *engage.v*, the **Act** FE appears in the syntactic locality of the LU, usually as a dependent. Phrases like *engage in friendship with someone* would have the prepositional phrase following the verb annotated with the **Act** FE tag. However, in the `Forming_relationships` frame, such an FE would not appear because the LUs evoking this frame – such as *befriend.v*, for example – already encode the **Act**. In other frames inheriting `Intentionally_act`, however, such as the `Daring` and the `Confronting_problems` frames, there will be a core FE inheriting the **Act** FE, namely, the **Action** and the **Issue** FEs, respectively.

When the prompt is modified so that the word "unexpressed" is erased – see (55) – the answer includes an FE inheriting the **Attribute** FE, as in (56a). We also conducted the same test with OpenAssistant to assess whether the removal of "unexpressed" would have any impact on the performance.

(55)   USER: There is a semantic frame for "gradable attributes", whose definition is as follows: "An Entity has an implicit Value for an Attribute. Degree expresses either explicit comparison or the deviation of the Value when compared with other entities of similar kind. The Value may hold only relative to a particular Time or in particular Circumstances.". Core frame elements in this frame are "Entity", "Degree", "Attribute" and "Value". The "color" frame inherits the "gradable attributes" frame. Core frame elements in the "color" frame are "Entity" and "Color". The "color" frame is evoked by adjectives such as "azure", "beige", "blue", "orange", "pink", "red", among others. Now, propose other semantic frames inheriting the "gradable attributes" frame. Present them as a table in which columns are "Frame Name", "Frame Definition", "Frame Elements", "Frame Element Definition", "Words evoking the frame".

(56)   a. ChatGPT: Sure, here's a table with some proposed semantic frames that inherit the "gradable attributes" frame, as well as their definitions, frame elements, element definitions, and words that might evoke the frame:

Frame Name	Frame Definition	Frame Elements	Frame Element Definition	Words Evoking the Frame
Temperature	An Entity has a temperature that can be compared to other entities of a similar kind or vary depending on circumstances.	Entity, Degree, Temperature	Entity refers to the object with a temperature, Degree expresses the temperature in a specific unit (e.g. Celsius, Fahrenheit), Temperature refers to the degree of hotness or coldness	Hot, cold, warm, cool, icy
Loudness	An Entity has a sound volume that can be compared to other entities of a similar kind or vary depending on circumstances.	Entity, Degree, Volume	Entity refers to the object producing a sound, Degree expresses the volume level in a specific unit (e.g. decibels), Volume refers to the degree of sound intensity	Quiet, loud, soft, noisy, hushed
Speed	An Entity has a speed that can be compared to other entities of a similar kind or vary depending on circumstances.	Entity, Degree, Speed	Entity refers to the object moving at a certain speed, Degree expresses the speed in a specific unit (e.g. miles per hour, kilometers per hour), Speed refers to the degree of swiftness	Fast, slow, quick, brisk, leisurely
Size	An Entity has a size that can be compared to other entities of a similar kind or vary depending on circumstances.	Entity, Degree, Size	Entity refers to the object with a certain size, Degree expresses the size in a specific unit (e.g. inches, meters), Size refers to the degree of magnitude	Big, small, large, tiny, huge

Brightness	An Entity has a brightness that can be compared to other entities of a similar kind or vary depending on circumstances.	Entity, Degree, Brightness	Entity refers to the object with a certain brightness, Degree expresses the brightness in a specific unit (e.g. lumens), Brightness refers to the degree of luminosity	Bright, dim, radiant, gloomy, shining

Note that these are just a few examples, and there could be many more semantic frames that inherit the "gradable attributes" frame. The exact definitions and frame elements may also vary depending on the specific context and usage.

b. OpenAssistant:

Frame Name	Frame Definition	Frame Elements	Frame Element Definition	Words Evoking the Frame
Loudness	An Object emits a Sound that can be Measured on a Scale between Silence and Very Loud.	Amplitude	Volume, Intensity	loud, soft, quiet, booming, deafening
Weight	An Object has a Mass that can be Measured on a Scale.	Mass	Heavy, light	heavy, light, dense, flimsy
Speed	Motion can be Measured on a Range between Static and Fast.	Velocity	Slow, fast, rapid, sluggish	slow, quick, fast, brisk
Temperature	Thermal Energy can be Measured on a Scale between Cold and Hot.	Energy	Cool, warm, cold, hot, freezing, scorching	cool, warm, chilly, steamy, icy, blazing
Humidity	Moisture Content can be Measured on a Scale between Dry and Wet.	Water Content	Arid, humid, damp, soggy, parched, saturated	dry, wet, moist, clammy, sticky, waterlogged

The new prompt configuration presented in (55) causes an improvement in the answer provided by both OpenAssistant and ChatGPT. The FE names proposed by OpenAssistant are now more consistent with the types found in FrameNet. As for ChatGPT, there is also improvement in (56a), when checked against FrameNet definitions, such as the definition of Size, for example. But FrameNet considers the **Degree** FE for Size as noncore, while ChatGPT, in (56a), defines it as core. On the other hand, in FrameNet's definition of the Temperature frame, the list of core FEs includes both **Attribute** and **Temperature**, because the valency of adjectives evoking this frame, such as *cold.a* and *hot.a*, may make room for both of **Attribute** and **Temperature** FEs in sentences such as (57), where the **Attribute** FE is incorporated in the adjective stem and the **Temperature** FE is represented by the number phrase.

(57)   It's already fall and it's [38°C$_{\text{Temperature}}$] [hot$_{\text{Attribute}}$] in Brazil still!

The types of mistakes ChatGPT and OpenAssistant make when proposing frames inheriting the Gradable_attributes frame are a consequence of the fact that proposing a new frame does not rely solely on the abstraction of distributional patterns of lexical items. It also requires an analysis of the prototypical, culturally grounded scene any speaker of the target language will learn in their journey towards becoming proficient in that language. The fact that the performances of the chatbots seem to be better in the previous experiment points to an inverse correlation between the success of the chatbot as a copilot and the descriptive power of FrameNet. In other words, because Frame Semantics bases its analyses on the valency patterns shown by lexical items, frames for words of a more predicative nature tend to be more complex than the ones for entities.

In the next section, we analyze the performance of AI LLM chatbots for eventive frames.

6.5 Experiment 5: Eventive Frame Building

Frames modeling events constitute the majority of FrameNet. Among the circa 1,200 frames in Berkeley FN data release 1.7, 646 are related to the Event frame. Like the Entity and the Attribute frames, the Event frame is very general. It features three core FEs: **Place**, **Time**, and **Event**, the last being core unexpressed. This configuration models the fact that events are dynamic states of affairs that develop over time somewhere. In fact, the LUs, even the verbs, evoking the Event frame in English – see Figure 12 – conform to this definition. They either take the **Event** FE as their external argument or incorporate it to their stems, and they at least presuppose some inferable **Time** and **Place**.

Figure 12 also lists the frames inheriting Event. They can be further divided into two clusters. The first of them includes the frames that will serve as the centers for networks of subtypes of events. Eventive_affecting, Intentionally_act, Motion, and Objective_influence – this last one shown in Figure 13 – are in this cluster. The frames inheriting them define configurations of semantic roles that, at least in some languages such as English and Brazilian Portuguese, serve as the semantic poles of argument

Figure 12 The Event frame in FrameNet.

Figure 13 The `Objective_influence` frame in FrameNet.

structure constructions. The `Transitive_action` frame, inheriting the `Objective_influence` frame, is one such case, as can be seen in Figure 14. The second cluster includes frames with smaller inheritance networks.

Following our pattern in Experiments 3 and 4, we chose to prompt ChatGPT and OpenAssistant with frames inheriting `Event`. However, this time, we experimented with two levels of inheritance and conducted the

Transitive_action

Figure 14 The `Transitive_action` frame in FrameNet.

experiment with both the first-level inheritance frame, namely, `Objective_influence`, and the second-level inheritance frame, namely, `Transitive_action`. The reason behind this choice is the difference between those two frames in terms of FE complexity and LU productivity. While `Objective_influence` has many core unexpressed FEs, which are not inherited by one of its daughter frames – `Transitive_action` – but are present in the other daughter frame – `Control` – it is also evoked by many LUs. Yet, the basic FE configuration of `Transitive_action` is kept in the daughter frames inheriting it, although the lack of LUs evoking it may compromise the performance of the AI LLM chatbot. Here, we report on the results for the experiments with the `Transitive_action` frame, since they were better.

We used the same prompt configurations tested so far; that is, we experimented both with the maintenance of the separation between core and core unexpressed FEs, and with merging all core FEs under the "core" label. The performance of both chatbots was considerably better when prompted with the `Transitive_action` frame and, therefore, those are the chat sequences we will report on next. The prompts we gave to the chatbots and the answers given by them are presented next. We report the prompts in (58) and (62); each was given to both ChatGPT and OpenAssistant in a new chat instance to preclude previous prompts to the model from influencing the results. Because the answers presented problems in all cases, we asked the chatbots to correct their mistakes.

The first prompt configuration kept the distinction between core and core unexpressed FEs in the `Transitive_action` frame and included the LUs evoking the `Destroying` frame. As already indicated, there was a need to ask the LLMs to correct their proposals. The beginning of the dialogue is reproduced in (58–59).

(58)　　USER: There is a semantic frame for "transitive action", whose definition is as follows: "This frame characterizes, at a very abstract level, an Agent or Cause affecting a Patient. This frame is inherited by many lower-level frames.". Core frame elements in this frame are "Agent" and "Patient". Core unexpressed frame elements are "Cause" and "Event". The "destroying" frame inherits the "transitive action" frame. Core frame elements in the "destroying" frame are "Cause", "Destroyer" and "Patient". The "destroying" frame is evoked by verbs such as "annihilate", "blast", "blow up", "demolish", "destroy", "devastate", "lay waste", "level", "obliterate", "raze", "ruin", "take out", "unmake" and "vaporize", and by the nouns "annihilation", "demolition", "destruction", "devastation", "dismantle", "dismantlement" and "obliteration". Now, propose other semantic frames inheriting the "transitive action" frame. Present them as a table in which columns are "Frame Name", "Frame Definition", "Frame Elements", "Frame Element Definition", "Words evoking the frame".

(59)   a. ChatGPT: Here is a table of additional semantic frames that inherit the "transitive action" frame:

Frame Name	Frame Definition	Frame Elements	Frame Element Definition	Words Evoking the Frame
Creating	This frame characterizes an Agent or Cause producing a Patient.	Agent, Patient	Agent is the entity causing the creation, and Patient is the entity being created.	Create, make, produce, generate, develop, form, build, construct, design
Cooking	This frame characterizes an Agent preparing a Patient as food.	Agent, Patient	Agent is the entity preparing the food, and Patient is the food being prepared.	Cook, bake, roast, grill, fry, sauté, boil, simmer, stew
Healing	This frame characterizes an Agent or Cause curing a Patient.	Agent, Patient	Agent is the entity performing the healing, and Patient is the entity being healed.	Heal, cure, treat, remedy, fix, mend, restore, alleviate, soothe
Teaching	This frame characterizes an Agent or Cause imparting knowledge to a Patient.	Agent, Patient	Agent is the entity doing the teaching, and Patient is the entity being taught.	Teach, instruct, educate, train, coach, tutor, mentor, enlighten, guide
Moving	This frame characterizes an Agent or Cause changing the position or location of a Patient.	Agent, Patient	Agent is the entity causing the movement, and Patient is the entity being moved.	Move, shift, transport, carry, transfer, relocate, displace, migrate, haul
Cleaning	This frame characterizes an Agent or Cause removing dirt or impurities from a Patient.	Agent, Patient	Agent is the entity doing the cleaning, and Patient is the entity being cleaned.	Clean, wash, scrub, mop, sweep, dust, vacuum, sanitize, disinfect

Note that the frame elements and definitions may vary depending on the specific semantics of each frame. The words evoking the frame are not exhaustive but represent some common examples.

b. OpenAssistant:

Frame Name	Frame Definition	Frame Elements	Frame Element Definition	Words Evoking the Frame
Transitive Action	An abstract frame characterizing an agent/cause affecting a patient	Agent	Person or thing performing the action	destroy, harm, damage, impact, influence
Destroying	Inherited from Transitive Action; characterized by cause, destroyer, & patient	Cause	Reason or mechanism for the action	annihilate, blast, blow up, demolish, destroy, devastate, lay waste, level, obliterate, raze, ruin, take out, unmake, vaporize
Helping	Transitive action where goal is assistance rather than harmful change	Assistant	Person or entity providing aid	assist, benefit, cooperate, contribute, facilitate, guide, render service, support
Competing	Transitive action with mutually exclusive goals between agents	Competitor 1	First party involved in competition	challenge, contend, contend against, dispute, fight, oppose, vie with
Compromising	Transitive action resulting in agreement through concession	Negotiator	Person engaged in negotiation	arbitrate, barter, bargain, conciliate, mediate, reconcile
Collaborating	Transitive action involving multiple parties working together towards shared goal	Partner	Party participating in collaboration	ally, associate, confederate, join forces with
Teaching	Transitive action aimed at imparting knowledge or skill	Educator	Person responsible for education	coach, educate, instruct, train
Healing	Transitive action intended to alleviate injury or disease	Healer	Person who provides healing care	cure, mend, nurse, remedy, restore, treat

Both chatbots make mistakes in their responses to the prompt in (58). Both of them propose frames with missing FEs, which would be profiled by LUs in frames for "healing" and "teaching." ChatGPT makes one additional mistake concerning FEs: Instead of proposing names that highlight that FEs are micro-thematic functions directly anchored in the scene described by the frames, it repeats "Agent" and "Patient" as the names of all FEs. On the other hand, OpenAssistant starts its answer by repeating the `Transitive_action` and the `Destroying` frames, which were present in the prompt. Because the mistakes are different in nature, the continuation of the chat was also different. We start with ChatGPT in (60–61).

(60)   USER: There seems to be a problem with some of the frames you suggested. The lexical units you proposed for the frames "healing", "teaching", "moving," and "cleaning" usually profile not only Agent and Patient, but also other frame elements. For example, the "Healing" frame would involve other frame elements, such as the Medication. Moreover, in FrameNet, frame element names tend to be more specific to the frame. So, instead of Agent, the "Healing" frame would feature a Healer frame element. Please revise the definitions you proposed above.

(61)   ChatGPT: Thank you for pointing that out. Here are revised definitions for the frames, incorporating additional frame elements and more specific definitions for existing ones:

Frame Name	Frame Definition	Frame Elements	Frame Element Definition	Words Evoking the Frame
Creating	This frame characterizes an Agent or Cause producing a Patient.	Agent, Patient, Instrument	Agent is the entity causing the creation, Patient is the entity being created, and Instrument is the tool or material used to create the Patient.	Create, make, produce, generate, develop, form, build, construct, design
Cooking	This frame characterizes an Agent preparing a Patient as food.	Chef, Food, Instrument, Means	Chef is the entity preparing the food, Food is the food being prepared, Instrument is the tool used to cook, and Means are the ingredients used to cook the food.	Cook, bake, roast, grill, fry, sauté, boil, simmer, stew

Healing	This frame characterizes an Agent or Cause curing a Patient.	Healer, Patient, Instrument, Means	Healer is the entity performing the healing, Patient is the entity being healed, Instrument is the tool used for healing, and Means are the methods or treatments used to heal the Patient.	Heal, cure, treat, remedy, fix, mend, restore, alleviate, soothe
Teaching	This frame characterizes an Agent or Cause imparting knowledge to a Student.	Teacher, Student, Knowledge, Means	Teacher is the entity doing the teaching, Student is the entity being taught, Knowledge is the information being imparted, and Means are the methods used to teach the Student.	Teach, instruct, educate, train, coach, tutor, mentor, enlighten, guide
Moving	This frame characterizes an Agent or Cause changing the position or location of an Entity.	Mover, Entity, Instrument, Path	Mover is the entity causing the movement, Entity is the entity being moved, Instrument is the tool or means used to move the Entity, and Path is the trajectory of the movement.	Move, shift, transport, carry, transfer, relocate, displace, migrate, haul
Cleaning	This frame characterizes an Agent or Cause removing dirt or impurities from a Surface.	Cleaner, Surface, Instrument	Cleaner is the entity doing the cleaning, Surface is the entity being cleaned, and Instrument is the tool or means used to clean the Surface.	Clean, wash, scrub, mop, sweep, dust, vacuum, sanitize, disinfect

Note that these definitions are not exhaustive and may vary depending on the context and usage of the words. The words evoking the frame are also not exhaustive but represent some common examples.

In general, the frame candidates proposed by ChatGPT when prompted with the Transitive_action frame are good. As can be seen in (61), all candidate frames proposed indicate a subtype of transitive action,

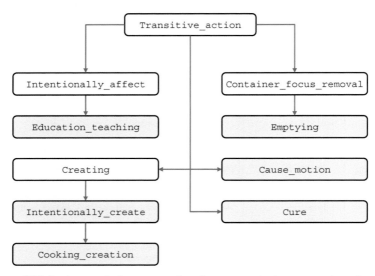

Figure 15 Inheritance chains connecting the `Transitive_action` frame to existing FrameNet frames, which are similar to the ones proposed by ChatGPT in (61). Similar frames are marked with a gray background.

although at a different level of granularity. FrameNet has frames for `Intentionally_create`, `Cooking_creation`, `Cure`, `Education_teaching`, `Cause_motion`, and `Emptying`, which would be very similar to the candidate frames proposed, respectively. Some of them are directly related to `Transitive_action`, while others are in an inheritance chain leading to this frame. Such a configuration is shown in Figure 15.

However, we did notice that, contrary to FrameNet methodology, the chatbot failed to name the FEs mnemonically or to indicate their specificity to the frame proposed. Additionally, some of the frames proposed lacked core FEs. We corrected the LLM in (60) and, as shown in (61), the result was that, in some cases, the list of FEs improved, as in the responses for the "Healing," "Teaching," and "Moving" frames. In others, the addition of an Instrument FE was inadequate.

Here is the remainder of the conversation with OpenAssistant:

(62)   USER: There seems to be a problem with some of the frames you suggested. The lexical units you proposed for the frames "healing", "teaching", "helping," and "competing" usually profile not only one frame element, but also other frame elements. For example, the "Healing" frame would involve other frame elements, such as the Medication. Moreover, you repeated the "Transitive action" and the "Destroying" frames, which were already present in the prompt. Please revise the definitions you proposed above.

(63)   OpenAssistant:

Frame Name	Frame Definition	Frame Elements	Frame Element Definitions	Words Evoking the Frames
Transitive Action	Characterization of an event that involves an agent causing a state change in a patient	Agent (Person or Thing causing the action)	Patient (Object receiving the action)	Act, alter, ameliorate, annihilate, assassinate, assault, attack, benight, break down, change, convert, corrupt, crush, decompose, debase, defeat, defile, dent, disintegrate, dominate, execute, exhaust, harm, interdict, kill, maim, neutralize, plague, pulverize, ravage, reduce, undermine, vanquish
Help	Assistance provided by an agent to another person or object	Helper (The provider of help)	Beneficiary (The recipient of help)	Abet, aid, attend, benefactor, bolster, brother-keeper, champion, comfort, enable, feed, foster, furnish, generate, husbandman, protect, redeem, succor, supplement
Education	Process of acquiring knowledge and skills	Educator (Teacher or trainer)	Student (Learner)	Acquire, apprenticed, assimilate, coach, counsel, discipline, enlighten, indoctrinate, initiate, learn, mastery, monitor, scholarship, study, teach, tutor, upgrade, wisdom
Healing	Restoration of health after illness or injury	Healer (Medical professional)	Diseased person or injured body part	Ameliorate, antidote, assuage, balm, bedside manner, boon, breathe life into, bring around, bruise, cater to, charm, chiropract, comfort, consult, cure, diagnose, ease pain, fix, fortify, hospitality, lenience, loom over, medical examination, narcotic, nurse back to health, operate, patch up, pharmacopoeia, physician, prescribe medicine, rectification, rescue, set broken bones, stitch wounds, surgery, therapy, treatment

When OpenAssistant was instructed to correct itself, it proposed relevant second FEs, but presented them in the wrong column, namely the one where FE definitions should be presented. It also augmented the list of LUs and, although some of them are adequate to the candidate frames, many others are not.

Finally, we repeated the prompt based on the `Transitive_action` frame but, this time, without mentioning that some core FEs were unexpressed. The resulting dialogue is shown in (64–65).

(64)   USER: There is a semantic frame for "transitive action", whose definition is as follows: "This frame characterizes, at a very abstract level, an Agent or Cause affecting a Patient. This frame is inherited by many lower-level frames.". Core frame elements in this frame are "Agent", "Patient", "Cause" and "Event". The "destroying" frame inherits the "transitive action" frame. Core frame elements in the "destroying" frame are "Cause", "Destroyer" and "Patient". The "destroying" frame is evoked by verbs such as "annihilate", "blast", "blow up", "demolish", "destroy", "devastate", "lay waste", "level", "obliterate", "raze", "ruin", "take out", "unmake" and "vaporize", and by the nouns "annihilation", "demolition", "destruction", "devastation", "dismantle", "dismantlement" and "obliteration". Now, propose other semantic frames inheriting the "transitive action" frame. Present them as a table in which columns are "Frame Name", "Frame Definition", "Frame Elements", "Frame Element Definition", "Words evoking the frame".

(65)   a. ChatGPT:

Frame Name	Frame Definition	Frame Elements	Frame Element Definition	Words Evoking the Frame
Causing harm	This frame characterizes an Agent or Cause affecting a Patient in a negative or harmful way.	Agent, Patient, Cause, Event	Agent: The entity causing the harm. Patient: The entity being harmed. Cause: The reason or motive behind the harm. Event: The act or occurrence of causing harm.	Harm, Injure, Hurt, Damage, Wound, Afflict, Corrupt, Infect, Poison, Sicken, Taint, Contaminate
Creating	This frame characterizes an Agent bringing a new object or entity into existence.	Agent, Object, Event	Agent: The entity creating something. Object: The entity being created. Event: The act or occurrence of creating.	Build, Construct, Design, Develop, Fashion, Form, Invent, Make, Manufacture, Produce, Shape

Moving	This frame characterizes an Agent causing a Patient to change its location.	Agent, Patient, Destination, Event	Agent: The entity causing the movement. Patient: The entity being moved. Destination: The location to which the Patient is moved. Event: The act or occurrence of moving.	Carry, Drag, Haul, Lift, Pull, Push, Shift, Transport, Transfer
Transforming	This frame characterizes an Agent or Cause changing the nature, form, or state of a Patient.	Agent, Patient, Cause, Result, Event	Agent: The entity causing the transformation. Patient: The entity being transformed. Cause: The reason or motive behind the transformation. Result: The entity resulting from the transformation. Event: The act or occurrence of transforming.	Alter, Change, Convert, Modify, Mutate, Renew, Shift, Transfigure, Transmute, Turn

These are just a few examples of semantic frames that could inherit the "transitive action" frame. There are many other possible frames depending on the context and the specific language being used.

b. OpenAssistant:

Frame Name	Frame Definition	Frame Elements	Frame Element Definition	Words Evoking the Frame
Transitive Action	An agent acting on a patient	Agent	Something performing an action	Destroyer, Patient
Conveying	Agent conveys something (e.g., idea) to recipient	Agent, Recipient	Someone who performs an action	Communicator, Receptor
Helping	Agent helps someone/ something in need	Helper, Needy	One providing assistance	Assistant, Supporter

Making	Agent produces something tangible from materials	Producer, Materials	Someone creating something	Artisan, Manufacturer
Learning	Person acquires knowledge/skills through experience/ instruction	Learner, Educator	Somebody gaining understanding	Scholar, Teacher
Giving	Agent gives something valuable to recipient	Donor, Receiver	Someone generously transferring ownership	Benefactor, Recipient
Challenging	Agent presents obstacle or competition for another	Challenger, Opponent	Someone posing a challenge	Contender, Adversary

Once again, both chatbots make mistakes when proposing candidate frames, and once again the mistakes are of a different nature. ChatGPT includes an **Event** FE in all of the proposed frames. OpenAssistant, in turn, includes two transfer frames – "Giving" and "Conveying" – among the ones suggested, without naming the theme. Also, the LUs proposed by OpenAssistant do not include any verbs. Because of that, we proceeded with the chat in different ways for each of the chatbots: (66–67) reports on the chat with ChatGPT, while (68–69) does the same for OpenAssistant.

(66)   USER: There seems to be a problem with some of the frames you suggested. The lexical units you proposed for the frames do not profile an Event frame element. Also, the "Moving" frame may involve other frame elements, such as the Source or the Path of the motion. Please revise the definitions you proposed above.

(67)   ChatGPT: Thank you for pointing that out. I apologize for the oversight. Here are revised definitions for the frames I proposed earlier:

Frame Name	Frame Definition	Frames	Frame Element Definition	Words Evoking the Frame
Causing harm	This frame characterizes an Agent or Cause affecting a Patient in a negative or harmful way.	Agent, Patient, Cause, Event	Agent: The entity causing the harm. Patient: The entity being harmed. Cause: The reason or motive behind the harm. Event: The act or occurrence of causing harm.	Harm, Injure, Hurt, Damage, Wound, Afflict, Corrupt, Infect, Poison, Sicken, Taint, Contaminate
Creating	This frame characterizes an Agent bringing a new object or entity into existence.	Agent, Object, Event	Agent: The entity creating something. Object: The entity being created. Event: The act or occurrence of creating.	Build, Construct, Design, Develop, Fashion, Form, Invent, Make, Manufacture, Produce, Shape
Moving	This frame characterizes an Agent causing a Patient to change its location.	Agent, Patient, Destination, Source, Path, Event	Agent: The entity causing the movement. Patient: The entity being moved. Source: The starting location of the movement. Destination: The final location of the movement. Path: The route taken between the Source and Destination. Event: The act or occurrence of moving.	Carry, Drag, Haul, Lift, Pull, Push, Shift, Transport, Transfer
Transforming	This frame characterizes an Agent or Cause changing the nature, form, or state of a Patient.	Agent, Patient, Cause, Result, Event	Agent: The entity causing the transformation. Patient: The entity being transformed. Cause: The reason or motive behind the transformation. Result: The entity resulting from the transformation. Event: The act or occurrence of transforming.	Alter, Change, Convert, Modify, Mutate, Renew, Shift, Transfigure, Transmute, Turn

I hope these revised definitions better capture the necessary frame elements and their definitions. Let me know if you have any further questions.

In the case of ChatGPT, for the experiment with the `Transitive_action` frame, the removal of the information about core unexpressed FEs resulted in worse results. Because the **Event** FE is not expressed in the frames inheriting `Transitive_action`, the removal of this information led the chatbot into proposing an inadequate **Event** FE in all the candidate frames. Such a mistake still happened after the correction indicated in (66).

(68)   USER: There seems to be a problem with some of the frames you suggested. The lexical units you proposed for the frames do not include any verbs. Also, the "Giving" and the "Conveying" frames may involve at least one other frame element, namely the Object being given or the Information being conveyed. Please revise the definitions you proposed above.

(69)   OpenAssistant: I apologize if my previous response was unclear or incomplete. Here's a revised version that includes verb forms and additional details where necessary:

Frame Name	Frame Definition	Frame Elements	Frame Element Definition	Verbs Evoking the Frame	Nouns Evoking the Frame
Transitive Action	Refers to actions performed by an agent upon a patient	Agent, Patient	Entity carrying out or receiving the action	Blow up, Demolish, Devastate, etc.	destruction, demolition, devastation
Conveying	Involves one entity conveying information to another	Source, Recipient	Agent responsible for conveying information	Communicate, Transfer, Inform, Relay, etc.	Communicator, Carrier, Transmitter, Informant
Helping	Focuses on assisting someone in need of aid	Help, Need	Agent offering support or assistance	Assistance, Support, Aid, Relief, etc.	helper, supporter, assistant, rescuer
Making	Reflects producing goods or objects using materials or raw substances	maker, material	Agent engaged in manufacturing processes	Create, Manufacture, Build, Form, etc.	Artifact, Commodity, Product, Creation
Learning	Describes the process of obtaining knowledge or skills	learner, teacher	Agent participating in education or instruction	Study, Absorb, Apprehend, Grasp, etc.	scholar, pupil, disciple, student

Giving	Concentrates on donating resources or possessions	Give, Donor, Receive, Acquire, etc.	Agent involved in gift exchange or allocation	Grant, Offer, Provide, Dispense, Endow, etc.	benefactor, contributor, provider, donor

As can be seen for OpenAssistant, the request for correction did not result in a proposal addressing the issues referring to the lack of a theme-like FE in the transfer frames. However, OpenAssistant created a new column in the table for proposing two separate lists of candidate LUs: one for verbs and one for nouns. The lists contain mostly good candidate LUs, which is a plus. However, the first row of the table still lists the Transitive_action frame, but, this time, with a list of LUs evoking the Destroying frame.

The results of the experiments with eventive frames reinforce the claim that small details in the prompt may generate important changes in the quality of the outcome proposed by the copilot. This is reinforced by the follow-up prompts requesting corrections. The chat history plays a key role in the answers proposed by AI LLM chatbots. They are designed this way so as to be able to emulate a dialogue. However, when told about their mistakes and prompted to offer a correction, they will still rely on such chat history. Their talkative nature is, therefore, both a feature and a bug for their deployment as copilots for linguists.

7 Final Safety Instructions: Risks and Limitations Revisited

Throughout this Element, we have proposed methods for responsibly deploying AI LLM chatbots in linguistic research. We pointed out how they can serve as eliciting interlocutors, and highlighted episodes where their brittleness and unreliability are evident. However, we have not, until now, explored their fabrication of nonsense in detail.

It is the case that AI LLM chatbots such as ChatGPT and OpenAssistant are built to chat. That is precisely what they do. They are not committed to the correctness of the content in the text they generate. In consequence, the analyses they propose conform to the prompt, not to the facts. To illustrate this claim in the context of this Element, consider the dialogue in (70–71).

(70)   USER: English has a construction named Inverted order, where the direct object of the verb can be used before the subject to indicate that the action performed

by the subject and affecting the object was unintentional. An example of this construction would be "The vase Mary broke". Please provide 10 additional examples of such construction and explain their meaning.

(71)   a. ChatGPT:·

The car John crashed – This sentence implies that John unintentionally crashed the car.

The glass Sarah dropped – This sentence suggests that Sarah did not intend to drop the glass.

The cake Tom burnt – This sentence indicates that Tom unintentionally burnt the cake.

The phone Emma lost – This sentence means that Emma did not intend to lose the phone.

The window Mark smashed – This sentence implies that Mark did not mean to smash the window.

The book Alex tore – This sentence suggests that Alex did not intend to tear the book.

The vase Lily knocked over – This sentence means that Lily did not intend to knock over the vase.

The picture Sam erased – This sentence indicates that Sam unintentionally erased the picture.

The plant Laura killed – This sentence implies that Laura did not mean to kill the plant.

The coffee Jane spilled – This sentence suggests that Jane did not intend to spill the coffee.

b. OpenAssistant:

Sure, here are ten examples of inverted order in English:

Example 1: The cup John dropped Meaning: The cup belonging to John fell due to him dropping it accidentally.

Example 2: The window Peter smashed Meaning: The glass panel got broken by Peter's actions.

Example 3: The phone Sarah lost Meaning: Sarah misplaced her mobile device.

Example 4: The plate Ruth chipped Meaning: Ruth carelessly damaged a ceramic plate.

Example 5: The key Bill locked inside Mean

Example 6: The book Mark read Meaning: Mark finished reading a book intentionally.

Example 7: The soup Lisa burnt Meaning: Lisa cooked some soup but burned it in the process.

Example 8: The curtains Tom ripped Meaning: Tom unintentionally tore part

Example9: The wall Tom hit his head on Meaning: Tom unintentionally collided his forehead with the wall while moving around in a cramped space.

Example 10: The alarm clock Jack snoozed Meaning: Jack pressed the snooze button on his alarm clock several times while trying to wake up.

The prompt in (70) states that English has a construction that it does not. Nonetheless, the models respond to it, providing the requested analysis. In other words, the models do not correct the user. This example is meant to demonstrate, via an extrapolation, that incorrect analyses in the prompt would be incorporated by the models in their answers. One could counterargue that other tools, such as Sketch Engine, for example, may also present data that may confuse the linguist. Nonetheless, in the case of Sketch Engine, the additional effort involved in querying the data – using a CQL, for example – puts an extra burden on the linguist, creating a delay in the work, and probably therefore, in practice, an extra safeguard against the inattentive acceptance of output. By contrast, easy chatting with an AI LLM chatbot perhaps invites ELIZA effects, seducing the linguist into inattentively accepting wrong analyses.

Additionally, proprietary tools, such as ChatGPT, are not transparent when it comes to either the training data used or the model's parameters. Fine-tuning for specific tasks is possible using an API, but highly constrained by OpenAI's practices and policies. For the researcher, these characteristics impair investigations into the limits of AI LLM chatbots as linguistic copilots and their potential risks. Moreover, the lack of access to all of the model components can hinder the development of tools to mitigate the risks generated by the model. In the context of using AI LLM chatbots as tools for scientific research, it is important that text automatically generated by these models be clearly identifiable. However, watermarking tools used to identify text generated by chatbots need access to the internal model parameters to be more accurate (Kirchenbauer et al., 2023). Proprietary models do not grant access to those parameters.

In short, the obscurity of ChatGPT prevents the linguist from controlling for important variables in the research. Hence, in this Element, we do not suggest that AI LLM chatbots, especially proprietary chatbots, are substitutes for corpus tools. The question is instead whether their robot performance can elicit insight from the linguist. Linguists often talk to each other about the problems they are working on, even before conducting a corpus study. It is common for a linguist to put forward a draft analysis to another linguist, who thinks about it and then comes back with a response, in minutes or maybe days or weeks, something like, "No, that can't be quite right, because … consider this example, in which …" Linguists indeed hold these conversations with themselves, working alone, putting forward a draft explanation ("Maybe it's because …") only to reject it thirty seconds later when they think of some other usage. In some sense, they knew about that other usage when they took their shot at a draft explanation, but they had not thought of it, considered it, weighed it. Dragging the work of masterful backstage cognition onstage is hard.

In the early days of machine translation, it was a source of great fun at linguistics conferences to quote howling mistakes made by a machine translation system. But machine translation systems like DeepL are now astonishingly useful, even though, with cunning, they can still be induced to make mistakes. We trust the trained linguist not to be misled by AI LLM chatbots. The question is instead whether such chatbots can serve as useful collaborative synthetic agents – with impressive powers not possessed by the linguist – in the industrious give and take of doing linguistics. Moreover, we believe that the deployment of AI LLM chatbots together with other tools – such as a corpus analysis software or a wizard-like tool like Lutma – may create a group of copilots for the linguist.

In this scenario, open source LLMs and the chatbots based on them, such as OpenAssistant, represent an advantage. Although their performance is still not the best, when compared to that of ChatGPT, they offer the linguist possibilities that proprietary models do not. First, they provide stability. Because linguists can choose the base model OpenAssistant uses, they can engage in comparative analyses that keep the training features stable. Second, as a consequence, linguists can investigate whether adding domain-specific material in the form of text to the training stage of those models improves their performance. For the experiments conducted in this Element, one could ask whether linearizing all FrameNet as text and feeding it as training data to the model would improve the performance in suggesting new LUs or whole new frames. Next, one could assess whether such an improvement was restricted to only the *style* of the answers provided, or extended additionally to the *content* of the proposed frames. The same idea could be applied to all constructions. Those questions are currently being investigated by us as we finish this Element, and will be reported at http://copilotsforlinguists.org.

8 Imagining the Future of Copilots for Linguists

AI systems that have been developed through machine learning are routinely trained on vast data, and AI models carry the traces of their training. In principle, they could be prompted to lay bare to the linguist patterns in the data they model. We forecast a future in which the linguist has an AI assistant, a sidekick, a copilot, to help form hypotheses, generate insights, develop models, and gather and analyze data. Hey, Assistant, propose, analyze, and exemplify the cognitive frames for *AI linguistics research assistant* ...

Assistants are not experts, but experts use them for what they are good for. The world of Ghiotto, Ghiberti, Verrocchio, Donatello, Verrocchio, Michelangelo, and Da Vinci – of art in general – employs studio assistants to achieve the master's design. Control of the team, and credit or blame for the outcome, rest with the master.

We find that although copilots can fail the linguist, they can also help substantially. They have been trained on ranges of data ludicrously beyond the capacities of a team of linguists to encounter, much less be aware of, much less analyze. They can consider data from any era, any culture, any language, including new situations. They can be tied to other repositories and tools, so that, as it were, they have their own stable of assistants. This is a prospect much to be desired. Copilots work constantly at superhuman speed, never tire, never complain, have no motive to cheat, have no motive to resist the direction of the master, can recall the history of a research conversation over any amount of text and any amount of time and distraction, do not pursue their own self-interest. They will work tirelessly in suggesting thoughts, possibilities, analyses, and evidence for the master's consideration.

But the linguist with a copilot has a new job: to learn how to prompt the copilot. The chattiness of the copilot, who accesses the history of the discourse, changes the experience of the linguist. But the linguist cannot just proceed to talk. The linguist must instead use language of the sort that will guide the copilot. Otherwise, the copilot will be useless. Learning this expert language will require transparency in the community: we will need to post entire chat histories that led to certain performances by the copilot, because the performance of the copilot in the local moment depends on the history of the chat, and we will need to analyze the patterns of prompt and responses, and locate best practices.

This Element outlines a research program: copilots for linguists. What is the current state of that practice, and how can we push that research program forward? Such a research program will develop very rapidly, with the advent of new machine learning techniques, new foundation models, new training of foundation models, and new APIs and plugins for existing copilots. We forecast the unification of Construction Grammar as a theoretical enterprise with the development of AI copilots derived from machine learning techniques. We have emphasized the all-important practice of prompt engineering for copilots. As human experts devise and refine prompts, templates for prompts, and scripts for prompting; as they inch forward with one gain after another, it would be useful to share a common forum for discussion. Accordingly, to serve all those who study copilots for

linguists, we have established a moderated discussion group at copilotsfor
linguists@case.edu, to which you may write to share reports of progress,
prospects, your participation in the project, and your request for membership. We have additionally established a website where we expect to post
progress and updates. It is http://copilotsforlinguists.org.

References

Almeida, V. G. 2016. Identificação Automática de Construções de Estrutura Argumental. MA thesis, Department of Linguistics, Federal University of Juiz de Fora, Juiz de Fora, Brazil.

Almeida, V. G. 2022. Modelagem e Identificação Automática de Construções de Estrutura Argumental: Uma proposta para o Constructicon da FrameNet Brasil. Ph.D. dissertation, Department of Linguistics, Federal University of Juiz de Fora, Juiz de Fora, Brazil.

Anwar, S., Ustalov, D., Arefyev, N., Ponzetto, S. P., Biemann, C., & Panchenko, A. 2019. HHMM at SemEval-2019 Task 2: Unsupervised frame induction using contextualized word embeddings. In *Proceedings of the 13th International Workshop on Semantic Evaluation*, Minneapolis, Minnesota (pp. 125–129). Association for Computational Linguistics.

Arefyev, N., Sheludko, B., Davletov, A., Kharchev, D., Nevidomsky, A., & Panchenko, A. 2019. Neural granny at SemEval-2019 Task 2: A combined approach for better modeling of semantic relationships in semantic frame induction. In *Proceedings of the 13th International Workshop on Semantic Evaluation* (pp. 31–38).

Bender, E. M. & Koller, A. 2020, July. Climbing towards NLU: On meaning, form, and understanding in the age of data. In *Proceedings of the 58th Annual Meeting of the Association for Computational Linguistics* (pp. 5185–5198).

Bender, E. M., Gebru, T., McMillan-Major, A., & Shmitchell, S. 2021. On the dangers of stochastic parrots: Can language models be too big? In *Proceedings of the 2021 ACM Conference on Fairness, Accountability, and Transparency* (pp. 610–623). New York: Association for Computing Machinery.

Bergen, B. & Binsted, K. 2015. Embodied grammar and humor. In Brône, G., Feyaerts, K., & Veale, T. (eds.), *Cognitive Linguistics and Humor Research* (pp. 49–68). Berlin: De Gruyter Mouton.

Birhane, A., Kasirzadeh, A., Leslie, D., et al. (2023). Science in the age of large language models. *Nature Reviews Physics*, 5: 277–280. https://doi.org/10.1038/s42254-023-00581-4.

Birhane, A., Prabhu, V. U., & Kahembwe, E. 2021. Multimodal datasets: Misogyny, pornography, and malignant stereotypes. arXiv preprint. arXiv:2110.01963.

Boas, H. C. 2005. Determining the productivity of resultative constructions: A reply to Goldberg and Jackendoff. *Language*, 81.2: 448–464.

Boas, H. C. 2013. Cognitive construction grammar. In Hoffmann, T. & Trousdale, G. (eds.), *The Oxford Handbook of Construction Grammar* (pp. 233–252). Oxford: Oxford University Press.

Boas, H. C. & Ziem, A. 2018. Constructing a constructicon for German. In Lyngfelt, B., Borin, L., Ohara, K., & Torrent, T. T. (eds.), *Constructicography: Constructicon Development across Languages* (pp. 83–228). Amsterdam: John Benjamins.

Bommasani, R., Hudson, D. A., Adeli, E., et al. 2021. On the opportunities and risks of foundation models. arXiv preprint. arXiv:2108.07258.

Bond, F. & Foster, R. 2013. Linking and extending an open multilingual wordnet. In *Proceedings of the 51st Annual Meeting of the Association for Computational Linguistics (Volume 1: Long Papers)* (pp. 1352–1362). Association for Computational Linguistics.

Brown, T., Mann, B., Ryder, N., et al. 2020. Language models are few-shot learners. *Advances in Neural Information Processing Systems*, 33: 1877–1901.

Chen, Brian X. 2023. We're using A.I. chatbots wrong: Here's how to direct them. *The New York Times*, July 20. www.nytimes.com/2023/07/20/technol ogy/personaltech/ai-chatgpt-bing-directions.html.

Coulson, S. 2001. *Semantic Leaps: Frame-Shifting and Conceptual Blending in Meaning Construction*. Cambridge: Cambridge University Press.

Croft, W. 2012. *Verbs: Aspect and Causal Structure*. Oxford. Oxford University Press.

Dannélls, D., Borin, L., & Heppin, K. H. 2021. *The Swedish FrameNet++: Harmonization, Integration, Method Development and Practical Language Technology Applications*. Amsterdam: John Benjamins Publishing Company.

Diessel, H. 2019. *The Grammar Network: How Linguistic Structure Is Shaped by Language Use*. Cambridge: Cambridge University Press.

Diniz da Costa, A., Gamonal, M. A., Paiva, V. M. R. L., et al. 2018. FrameNet-based modeling of the domains of tourism and sports for the development of a personal travel assistant application. In Torrent, T. T., Borin, L., & Baker, C. F. (eds.), *Proceedings of the Eleventh International Conference on Language Resources and Evaluation (LREC 2018)*, Miyazaki, Japan (pp. 6–12). Paris: ELRA.

Fauconnier, G. & Turner, M. 1996. Blending as a central process of grammar. In Goldberg, A. (ed.), *Conceptual Structure, Discourse, and Language* (pp. 113–130). Stanford: Center for the Study of Language and Information. [Expanded web version 1998, available at http://ssrn.com/ author=1058129.]

Fauconnier, G. & Turner, M. 2002. *The Way We Think: Conceptual Blending and the Mind's Hidden Complexities*. New York: Basic Books.

Fillmore, C. J. 1968. The case for case. In Bach, E. & Harms, R. T. (eds.), *Universals in Linguistic Theory* (pp. 1–88). New York: Holt, Rinehart and Winston.

Fillmore, C. J. 1976. Frame semantics and the nature of languages. In *Annals of the New York Academy of Sciences: Conference on the Origin and Development of Language and Speech*, 280: 20–32.

Fillmore, C. J. 1977a. Scenes-and-frames semantics. In Zampolli, A. (ed.), *Fundamental Studies in Computer Science*, number 59 (pp. 55–88). Amsterdam: North Holland Publishing.

Fillmore, C. J. 1977b. The need for a frame semantics in linguistics. In Karlgren, H. (ed.), *Statistical Methods in Linguistics*, volume 12 (pp. 5–29). Stockholm: Scriptor.

Fillmore, C. J. 1982. Frame semantics. In *Linguistics in the Morning Calm*. Linguistic Society of Korea (pp. 111–137). Seoul: Hanshin Publishing Company.

Fillmore, C. J. 1985. Frames and the semantics of understanding. *Quaderni di Semantica*, 6.2: 222–254.

Fillmore, C. J. 2008. The merging of "frames". In Rossini Favretti, R. (ed.), *Frames, Corpora, and Knowledge Representation* (pp. 1–12). Bologna: Bononia University Press.

Fillmore, C. J. 2013. Berkeley Construction Grammar. In Hoffmann, T. & Trousdale, G. (eds.), *The Oxford Handbook of Construction Grammar* (pp. 111–132). Oxford: Oxford University Press.

Fillmore, C. J. & Atkins, B. T. 1992. Towards a frame-based organization of the lexicon: The semantics of RISK and its neighbors. In Lehrer, A. & Kittay, E. (eds.), *Frames, Fields, and Contrast: New Essays in Semantics and Lexical Organization* (pp. 75–102). Hillsdale: Lawrence Erlbaum Associates, .

Fillmore, C. J. & Atkins, B. T. 1994. Starting where the dictionaries stop: The challenge for computational lexicography. In Atkins, B. T. S. & Zampolli, A. (eds.), *Computational Approaches to the Lexicon* (pp. 349–393). Oxford: Oxford University Press.

Fillmore, C. J., Kay, P., & O'Connor, M. C. 1988. Regularity and idiomaticity in grammatical constructions: The case of let alone. *Language*, 64.3: 501–538.

Fillmore, C. J., Johnson, C. R., & Petruck, M. R. 2003. Background to FrameNet. *International Journal of Lexicography*, 16.3: 235–250.

Goldberg, A. E. 1995. *Constructions: A Construction Grammar Approach to Argument Structure Constructions*. Chicago: University of Chicago Press.

Goldberg, A. E. 2006. *Constructions at Work*. Oxford: Oxford University Press.

Goldberg, A. E. 2019. *Explain Me This: Creativity, Competition, and the Partial Productivity of Constructions*. Princeton: Princeton University Press.

Gruzitis, N., Nespore-Berzkalne, G., & Saulite, B. 2018. Creation of Latvian FrameNet based on universal dependencies. In Torrent, T. T., Borin, L., &

Baker, C. F. (eds.), *Proceedings of the Eleventh International Conference on Language Resources and Evaluation (LREC 2018)*, Miyazaki, Japan (pp. 23–27). Paris: European Language Resources Association (ELRA).

Hahm, Y., Noh, Y., Han, J. Y., et al. 2020. Crowdsourcing in the development of a multilingual framenet: A case study of Korean FrameNet. In *Proceedings of the 12th Language Resources and Evaluation Conference*, Marseille, France (pp. 236–244). European Language Resources Association (ELRA).

Hartmann, S. & Gurevych, I. 2013. FrameNet on the way to Babel: Creating a bilingual FrameNet using Wiktionary as interlingual connection. In *Proceedings of the 51st Annual Meeting of the Association for Computational Linguistics (Volume 1: Long Papers)*, Sofia, Bulgaria (pp. 1363–1373). Association for Computational Linguistics.

Herbst, T. 2018. Collo-creativity and blending: Recognizing creativity requires lexical storage in constructional slots. *Zeitschrift für Anglistik und Amerikanistik*, 66.3: 309–326.

Hilpert, M. 2019. *Construction Grammar and Its Application to English*. 2nd ed. Edinburgh: Edinburgh University Press.

Hoffmann, T. 2022a. *Construction Grammar: The Structure of English* (Cambridge Textbooks in Linguistics). Cambridge: Cambridge University Press.

Hoffmann, T. 2022b. Constructionist approaches to creativity. *Yearbook of the German Cognitive Linguistics Association*, 101: 259–284.

Hoffmann, T. & Bergs, A. 2015. Are you a construction in disguise? Was Fußballgesänge uns über soziale und physische Kontexteigenschaften von Konstruktionen lehren. In Ziem, A. & Lasch, A. (eds.), *Konstruktionsgrammatik IV: Konstruktionen als soziale Konventionen und kognitive Routinen* (pp. 115–131). Tübingen: Stauffenburg.

Hoffmann, T. & Bergs, A. 2018. A Construction Grammar approach to genre. *CogniTextes*, 18: 1–27.

Hoffmann, T. & Bergs, A. 2024. Constructions all the way! Text types as constructions. In Hennemann, A. & Tacke, F. (eds.), *Diskurstraditionen – Konstruktionen – Genres* (Sprache in kulturellen Kontexten/Language in Cultural Contexts). Bonn: Bonn University Press.

Hoffmann, T. & Trousdale, G. (eds.) 2013. *The Oxford Handbook of Construction Grammar*. Oxford: Oxford University Press.

Hofstadter, D. R. 1995. Preface 4 the ineradicable Eliza effect and its dangers . In *Fluid Concepts and Creative Analogies: Computer Models of the Fundamental Mechanisms of Thought* (pp. 155–168). New York: Basic Books.

Kim, J., Hahm, Y., & Choi, K-S. 2016. Korean FrameNet expansion based on projection of Japanese FrameNet. In *Proceedings of COLING 2016, the 26th*

International Conference on Computational Linguistics: System Demonstrations, Osaka, Japan (pp. 175–179). The COLING 2016 Organizing Committee.

Kirchenbauer, J., Geiping, J., Wen, Y., Katz, J., Miers, I., & Goldstein, T. 2023. A watermark for large language models. *arXiv preprint*. arXiv:2301. 10226.

Leech, G. 2014. *The Pragmatics of Politeness*. Oxford: Oxford University Press.

Lowe, J. B., Baker, C. F., & Fillmore, C. J. 1997. A frame-semantic approach to semantic annotation. In *Proceedings of the ACL SIGLEX Workshop on Tagging Text with Lexical Semantics* (pp. 18–24). ACL.

Mahowald, K., Ivanova, A. A., Blank, I. A., Kanwisher, N., Tenenbaum, J. B., & Fedorenko, E. 2023. Dissociating language and thought in large language models: A cognitive perspective. *arXiv preprint*. arXiv:2301.06627.

Matos, E. E., Torrent, T. T., Almeida, V. G., et al. 2017. Constructional analysis using constrained spreading activation in a FrameNet-based structured connectionist model. In *The AAAI 2017 Spring Symposium on Computational Construction Grammar and Natural Language Understanding Technical Report SS-17-02* (pp. 222–229). Volume 17. Palo Alto, CA: AAAI Publications.

Ohara, K. H., Fujii, S., Ohori, T., Suzuki, R., Saito, H., & Ishizaki, S. 2004. The Japanese framenet project: An introduction. In *Proceedings of LREC-04 Satellite Workshop "Building Lexical Resources from Semantically Annotated Corpora"(LREC 2004)* (pp. 9–11). European Language Resources Association (ELRA).

Pavlick, E., Wolfe, T., Rastogi, P., Callison-Burch, C., Dredze, M., & Van Durme, B. 2015. FrameNet+: Fast paraphrastic tripling of FrameNet. In *Proceedings of the 53rd Annual Meeting of the Association for Computational Linguistics and the 7th International Joint Conference on Natural Language Processing (Volume 2: Short Papers)*, Beijing, China (pp. 408–413). Association for Computational Linguistics.

Pennacchiotti, M., De Cao, D., Basili, R., Croce, D., & Roth, M. 2008. Automatic induction of FrameNet lexical units. In *Proceedings of the 2008 Conference on Empirical Methods in Natural Language Processing* (pp. 457–465), Honolulu, HI. Association for Computational Linguistics.

Perek, F. & Lemmens, M. 2010. Getting at the meaning of the English at-construction: The case of a constructional split. *CogniTextes* 5. http:// cognitextes.revues.org/331.

QasemiZadeh, B., Petruck, M. R., Stodden, R., Kallmeyer, L., & Candito, M. 2019. SemEval-2019 task 2: Unsupervised lexical frame induction. In *Proceedings of the 13th International Workshop on Semantic Evaluation*.

Minneapolis, Minnesota (pp. 16–30). Association for Computational Linguistics.

Ribeiro, E., Mendonça, V., Ribeiro, R., et al. 2019, June. L2F/INESC-ID at SemEval-2019 task 2: Unsupervised lexical semantic frame induction using contextualized word representations. In *Proceedings of the 13th International Workshop on Semantic Evaluation* (pp. 130–136).

Rogers, A. 2021. Changing the world by changing the data. *arXiv preprint*. arXiv:2105.13947v1.

Rogers, A., Kovaleva, O., & Rumshisky, A. 2020. A primer in BERTology: What we know about how BERT works. In *Transactions of the Association for Computational Linguistics* (Vol. 8, pp. 842–866). ACL. https://doi.org/10.1162/tacl_a_00349.

Ruane, E., Birhane, A., & Ventresque, A. 2019. Conversational AI: Social and ethical considerations. In *AICS* (pp. 104–115).

Ruppenhofer, J., Ellsworth, M., Petruck, M. R. L., Johnson, C. R., Baker, C. F., & Scheffczyk, J. 2016. *FrameNet II: Extended theory and practice*. Berkeley, CA: ICSI.

Sampaio, T. F. 2010. A Família de Construções de Argumento Cindido no Português do Brasil. Ph.D. dissertation, Department of Linguistics, Federal University of Juiz de Fora, Juiz de Fora, Brazil.

Stefanowitsch, A. 2013. Collostructional analysis. In Hoffmann, T. & Trousdale, G. (eds.), *The Oxford Handbook of Construction Grammar* (pp. 290–306). Oxford: Oxford University Press.

Subirats, C. & Petruck, M. 2003. Surprise: Spanish FrameNet. In *Proceedings of CIL*, Prague (Vol. 17, p. 188).

Torrent, T. T., Salomão, M. M. M., da Silva Matos, E. E., et al. 2014. Multilingual lexicographic annotation for domain-specific electronic dictionaries: The Copa 2014 FrameNet Brasil project. *Constructions and Frames*, 6:1: 73–91.

Torrent, T. T., Matos, E. E. D. S., Belcavello, F., et al. 2022a. Representing context in FrameNet: A multidimensional, multimodal approach. *Frontiers in Psychology*, 13: 573.

Torrent, T. T., Almeida, A. L., Matos, E. E., Belcavello, F., Viridiano, M., & Gamonal, M. A. 2022b. Lutma: A frame-making tool for collaborative FrameNet development. In *Proceedings of the 1st Workshop on Perspectivist Approaches to NLP*, Marseille, France (pp. 100–107). European Language Resources Association (ELRA).

Touvron, H., Lavril, T., Izacard, G., et al. (2023). Llama: Open and efficient foundation language models. *arXiv preprint*. arXiv:2302.13971.

Turner, M. 1987. *Death is the Mother of Beauty: Mind, Metaphor, Criticism.* Chicago, IL: University of Chicago Press.

Turner, M. 1998. Figure. In Cacciari, C., Gibbs, Jr., R., & Katz, A. (eds.), *Figurative Language and Thought* (pp. 44–87). Oxford: Oxford University Press.

Turner, M. 2015. Blending in language and communication. In Dąbrowska, E. & Divjak, D. (eds.), *Handbook of Cognitive Linguistics* (pp. 211–232). Berlin: De Gruyter Mouton.

Turner, M. 2020. Constructions and creativity. *Cognitive Semiotics*, 13:1. https://doi.org/10.1515/cogsem-2020-2019.

Ungerer, T. & Hartmann, S. 2023. *Constructionist Approaches: Past, Present, Future.* (Cambridge Elements in Construction Grammar). Cambridge: Cambridge University Press.

van Dis, E. A. M., Bollen, J., Zuidema, W., van Rooij, R., & Bockting, C. L. 2023. ChatGPT: Five priorities for research. Conversational AI is a game-changer for science. Here's how to respond. *Nature*, 614: 224–226.

Yamada, K., Sasano, R., & Takeda, K. 2021. Semantic frame induction using masked word embeddings and two-step clustering. In *Proceedings of the 59th Annual Meeting of the Association for Computational Linguistics and the 11th International Joint Conference on Natural Language Processing (Volume 2: Short Papers)* (pp. 811–816). Association for Computational Linguistics.

Yong, Z. X. & Torrent, T. T. 2020. Semi-supervised deep embedded clustering with anomaly detection for semantic frame induction. In *Proceedings of the 12th Language Resources and Evaluation Conference*, Marseille, France (pp. 3509–3519). European Language Resources Association (ELRA).

You, L. & Liu, K. 2005. Building Chinese FrameNet database. In *2005 International Conference on Natural Language Processing and Knowledge Engineering*, Wuhan, China (pp 301–306). IEEE. https://doi.org/10.1109/NLPKE.2005.1598752.

Weissweiler, L., Hofmann, V., Köksal, A., & Schütze, H. 2022. The better your syntax, the better your semantics? Probing pretrained language models for the English comparative correlative. In *Proceedings of the 2022 Conference on Empirical Methods in Natural Language Processing*, December 7–11, 2022, Abu Dhabi, United Arab Emirates (pp. 10859–10882). Association for Computational Linguistics. https://aclanthology.org/2022.emnlp-main.746.pdf.

Acknowledgments

The authors acknowledge the support of the Case Western Research University High Performance Computing Cluster and the Case Western Reserve AI Strategy Group. NSF grant 2117439 provided computational resources. Torrent's research is funded by CNPq Research Productivity Grant no. 315749/2021–0. Almeida's research is funded by CAPES Grant no. 88887.816228/2023–00.

Cambridge Elements ☰

Construction Grammar

Thomas Hoffmann
Catholic University of Eichstätt-Ingolstadt

Thomas Hoffmann is Full Professor and Chair of English Language and Linguistics at the Catholic University of Eichstätt-Ingolstadt as well as Furong Scholar Distinguished Chair Professor of Hunan Normal University. His main research interests are usage-based Construction Grammar, language variation and change and linguistic creativity. He has published widely in international journals such as *Cognitive Linguistics, English Language and Linguistics*, and *English World-Wide*. His monographs *Preposition Placement in English* (2011) and *English Comparative Correlatives: Diachronic and Synchronic Variation at the Lexicon-Syntax Interface* (2019) were both published by Cambridge University Press. His textbook on *Construction Grammar: The Structure of English* (2022) as well as an Element on *The Cognitive Foundation of Post-colonial Englishes: Construction Grammar as the Cognitive Theory for the Dynamic Model* (2021) have also both been published with Cambridge University Press. He is also co-editor (with Graeme Trousdale) of *The Oxford Handbook of Construction Grammar* (2013, Oxford University Press).

Alexander Bergs
Osnabrück University

Alexander Bergs joined the Institute for English and American Studies at Osnabrück University, Germany, in 2006 when he became Full Professor and Chair of English Language and Linguistics. His research interests include, among others, language variation and change, constructional approaches to language, the role of context in language, the syntax/pragmatics interface, and cognitive poetics. His works include several authored and edited books (*Social Networks and Historical Sociolinguistics, Modern Scots, Contexts and Constructions, Constructions and Language Change*), a short textbook on *Synchronic English Linguistics*, one on *Understanding Language Change* (with Kate Burridge) and the two-volume *Handbook of English Historical Linguistics* (ed. with Laurel Brinton; now available as five-volume paperback) as well as more than fifty papers in high-profile international journals and edited volumes. Alexander Bergs has taught at the Universities of Düsseldorf, Bonn, Santiago de Compostela, Wisconsin-Milwaukee, Catania, Vigo, Thessaloniki, Athens, and Dalian and has organized numerous international workshops and conferences.

About the Series

Construction Grammar is the leading cognitive theory of syntax. The present Elements series will survey its theoretical building blocks, show how Construction Grammar can capture various linguistic phenomena across a wide range of typologically different languages, and identify emerging frontier topics from a theoretical, empirical and applied perspective.

Cambridge Elements ☰

Construction Grammar

Printed in the United States
by Baker & Taylor Publisher Services